Rune Correspondences

Frodi Ingsson

CONTENT

Thanks Óðinn

INTRODUCTION

This book is a collection of notes I've taken from over a hundred different Runic sources. This includes perspectives from academics, traditionalists, Armanists, new agers, feminists, gender fluid folk, occultists, fusionists, and others. Also included are correspondences from my guide, *Rune Yoga: Staða & Galdr*.

Everyone is different, and so everyone's experience of the Runes will be unique. To think otherwise runs counter to a common Heathen belief in self-determination: no one dictates what you believe or who you should be. In saying, I sought out as many different perspectives as possible to gain a deeper and more encompassing understanding of the Runes.

Other than my Rune Yoga correspondences, all the others in this book come from those referred to in the bibliography. I'm just sharing my notes, not endorsing any one view, belief, or association. The key is to find what resonates with you and use it to help you connect with the Runes.

Note on Rune Numbers: using Fehu as an example, 1:1 is saying 1st ætt: 1st Rune. The number after the slash is 1, for the first Rune of the Futhark. Othala is 3:8/24. Third aett: 8th Rune and the 24th Rune of the Futhark.

One translation for ætt is "family," and in the Runes there are three families (ættir) of eight Runes each.

Note on Correspondences: not all Runes will have an associated day, metal, celebration, or what have you. If you come across associations that are not present in the book, write them in, for that's what it's all about.

CONNECTING WITH THE RUNES

I connect with the Runes on three levels:
1. shape, sound, and meaning
2. Rune poems, stones, and artifacts
3. eddas, sagas, magical texts, and modern correspondences

Below is one path towards connecting with Tiwaz. Some of the things spoken of below came from this book, while other things came from further research as I wrote this section. Part of connecting with a Rune is finding your own path to it. This correspondence book is a great place to start, but don't let it be your only source. Read books, watch videos, have conversations, and take a journey down Google lane to see where the energy takes you.

First Level
(shape, sound, meaning)

For the first level I connect with a Rune through its staða (posture), galdr (intonation), and meaning (Tyr). The following Fehu video gives more information on this process.

www.youtube.com/watch?v=wFx8-gAx9Es

Second Level
(Rune poems, stones, and artifacts)

Old English
>   Tir is a guiding sign, traveling forth
>   it never fails, is always true,
>   keeping faith through night's gloom.

Norwegian
> Tyr is the one-handed among the Aesir;
> the smith is blowing often.

Icelandic
> Tyr is the one-hand god
> and the wolf's leavings
> and temple's protector.

Guiding, travel, faithful, true, Tyr and his story of offering his hand to Fenrir, smiths, and the temple's protector are some things mentioned in the poems. One association hinted at in the Old English poem is Tiwaz's connection to the north star, Polaris.

The Kylver Runestone has the Elder Futhark carved with multiple Tiwaz and Ansuz Runes stacked on top of one another as a bindrune. A bindrune is often used for magical purposes, as a type of sypher, or signature. This bindrune is believed to be a call to and request for Tyr and Óðinn to give victory, an association both gods share. The Runestone also has the palindrome "sueus," which has been proposed to be either connected with the horse or a specific Germanic tribe.

Sometimes carved Runes are not meant to say something, but rather are a magical operation, meditative practice, mental puzzle, galdr, or something else. When working with a magical action it could be something as simple as intoning the Runes' individual sounds such as S-U-E-U-S and paying attention to what comes up, or it could be some form of magical incantation where you intone the sound and say something powerful like, "May the sun's energy (S) and the oraches strength (U) give my horse (E) endurance (U) to the setting sun (S)."

The 6th century bracteate Seeland-II-C is a good example of a Rune artifact being used in a magical way to protect the wearer on a dangerous journey by increasing their chances/luck in being safe and successful. The magical galdr ends with a triple Tiwaz bindrune.

Level Three
(Eddas, sagas, magical texts, correspondences)

In "Sigrdrífumál" we first hear about Sigurðr's and Brynhild's story, and in chapter 20 of *The Volsung Saga* we get to learn more about the Runic spells Brynhild teaches Sigurðr.

List's Armanen Runes are sometimes connected with Óðinn's Rune spells. Tiwaz is associated with the 12th spell, which enables the Runologist to get answers from those hung and still swaying in the wind.

In the *Kreddur manuscript* there is a galdrastafur (magical stave) with a two-sided Tiwaz for protection against animal bites (go figure). It instructs the practitioner to scratch the symbols on oak and put it above the front door.

Some modern Tiwaz correspondences are guidance, clarity, finding meaning and purpose in life, justice, and victory.

Through learning and connecting with the different correspondences you have tapped into Tiwaz's energy. After that it's all about using the energy for whatever you want. One way to channel and use the energy is through ritual.

The following ritual comes from my guide, *Rune Yoga: Staða & Galdr*. This practice helps you use the Runic energies for some specific purpose. Let's say you are seeking guidance on something. It could be about a move, which job to take, relationships, or what to do about something.

Tiwaz Ritual-Meditation
- seek out isolation
- hallow out a space
- set intention or pose a question verbally
- ground yourself
- breathe and relax
- do a few Microcosmic Orbits
- when ready get in Tiwaz Staða
- breathe deeply and feel the energy flowing through you
- Galdr "t-t-t-t-t" while imagining and feeling the energy rising up the central energy channel, first sharp and loudly, but slowly intone quieter until the sound of "t's ending," like the air coming out of a tire goes into silence (allow that subtle sound to take you deep into the mind's space)
- rest in that silence and see what comes up

Through ritual you gain insights, epiphanies, actions to take, and ideas that will either answer your question, give you direction, or manifest what you seek. Things happen when you raise the energy and direct it towards a specific purpose.

Part of setting and raising the energy comes through intentional focus, working with the staða and galdr, and having objects connected to the Rune. To increase Tiwaz's energy use a greyish blue cloth or film in front of a candle (away from the flame of course) to give off that color frequency. Do the ritual when the sun is in Sagittarius or at least at night looking towards the north star, Polaris. Maybe do ritual while the moon is growing towards fullness. While hollowing out the space burn some sage and during the ritual offer Tyr some elderberry wine and have a drink or two yourself.

Having gathered the correspondence objects, raised the energy, invited Tyr, spoken your intention, and directed all the energy towards your aim, now sit or lay down and open yourself to whatever insights or things that come up.

After the ritual allow yourself to relax, come back into the body, breathe, reflect, enjoy the moment, and give thanks for the blessings in life.

To me magic is all about using energy to accomplish or fulfill a desire, intention, design, will, dream, need, or whatever. I've found things have their own unique energy, and when I combined the right energies with my intention and focus, magical things occur. This happens by connecting and incorporating those energies into myself while focusing my mind on whatever I'm seeking. By sustaining the focus and raising my energy and consciousness to the mind's eye, I've come to experience astral traveling, conscious expansion, gained insights, knowledge, increased synchronicities, found certainty, strength, power, and so much more.

CORREPONDENCES

Does a ruby, red, self-esteem, fire, or a full moon really have anything to do with Fehu? Are these associations real or psychological props?

I can tell you everything is composed of energy (physics), and that everything has its own vibrational expression. When one vibration interacts with another, something happens. It might not be big, but something does occur: an energy is exchanged. This energy can trigger thoughts, memories, emotions, sensations, insights, perspective shifts, elevated interactions, purposeful actions, life changes, and so much more.

I've learned through experience that things are connected. When those connections are tapped into magical things can happen. Change happens. Growth happens. Gaining wisdom and some control over life happens. And those things happen because the Runologist actively seeks to cultivate the self while gaining experience, understanding, and power.

A complete system of correspondences should touch in with major areas in life such as family, home, and money while also offering understandings, insights, and control over the self and the world around you. A good set of correspondences will help you connect with nature via associated animals, minerals, plants, trees, planets, stars, elements, seasons, times, and so on. The more you learn and connect with these things, the more their energies intertwine with your own. The correspondences should also offer meditative/ritualistic practices to help you connect with and cultivate different aspects of yourself. The Runes do all these things and more.

Some other benefits that come from working with the correspondences

- perceiving reality through Runic lens
- seeing from different perspectives
- connecting and experiencing different energies
- taking control of different facets of your life
- helping build skills, intelligence, insights, wisdom, connections
- assisting in self-cultivation and actualization
- offering an energetic way to accomplish your aims in life
- offering an energetic way to acquire and manifest things
- bringing awareness to and learning how to use life's patterns/cycles
- connecting with the Runic energies

The simplest way to work with the correspondences is to gather the associated materials you resonate with, research them, meditate with them, use them magically/ritualistically, and keep them around you as much as possible while paying attention to any unique thoughts, emotions, interactions, and experiences you have that are different than what you normally experience. As you connect with the Runes the insights and experiences gained will help you on your path.

Some things each Rune section will have

- pronunciation
- translated meaning
- number
- Rune poems
- positive and negative associations
- plant, tree, stone, animal, color, and other associated things
- time, season, celebration, direction, and element

- tarot and astrology connections
- myths, magical beings, and deities
- visualizations
- magical and meditative practices
- Rune Yoga practices

FEHU

Pronunciation: fay-hoo
Sound: *f* (*fee*)
Meaning: cattle, moveable wealth
Number: 1:1/1
Poems:

Old English
> Wealth is a comfort to all;
> share it well and be content,
> for the god's are watching.

Norwegian
> Wealth causes strife among kinsmen;
> the wolf feeds itself in the woods.

Icelandic
> Wealth causes strife among kin,
> and fire of the flood-tide
> and the serpent's way.

Ideograms: bovine horns, person reaching up and embracing life
Visualization: cattle in lush field
Divinities: Freya, Freyr, Auðumbla, Surt, Andvari, Njörðr
Eddas, Sagas, and Stories: Auðumbla, Siegfried's treasure, Gullveig's woe-workings, Gróttasöngr, the terrible sounding cow Sibilja (Saga of Ragnar Loðbrók chapters 9-10, 12), Hávamál 76-78, Thrymskvitha 23; Bosi and Herraud kill a slave and heifer to destroy ogress and her vulture for her wealth (The Saga of Bosi and Herraud ch.8)

Healing: circulatory, respiratory
Directions: south, east
Colors: red, golden red, bright red, yellowish red
Elements: fires, earth
Plants: marjoram, nettle, fennel, flax, lily of the valley
Trees: elder, ash, chestnut, beech, alder
Incense: frankincense
Gemstones: topaz, carnelian, green tourmaline, aventurine, amber, sunstone, citrine, ruby, blood agate, red jasper, garnet, sapphire, rose quartz
Metal: gold
Living Creatures: cattle, cat, swallow, linnet, boar, horse
Festivals: Summer Solstice, Almabtrieb
Holy Tide: Jól
Day: Saturday
Time of Day: 13:00, 12:30 PM to 1:30 PM
Time of Year: December 22nd – January 12th, June 29 – July 14
Moon Phase: full, new
Astrology: Aries, Venus, Moon
Tarot: Magician, Tower
Sacred Objects: Brísingamen, gold coins, gold ring, Horn of Plenty
Hall: Himinbjörg
Nine Worlds: Muspelheim
Zone: Cosmic Space
Magical Beings: firedrakes, fire giants, dragons, alchemical salamanders, fire spirits
Hávamál's Rune Poem (Ljóðatal): 146
Magical and Meditative Practices: increasing fertility, resources, and wealth, amplifying whatever one is working on, creating opportunities, kickstarting enterprises and intentions, perfecting skills and talents, protecting assets and interests, spells for abundance and love, protection against negative forces by inhaling strong electric currents and then exhaling explosive force while sending out arms in Runic shape,

strengthening psychic and intuitive abilities, letting go of fears, attracting celestial energies to enhance spiritual and occult skills, transferring energy, increasing power and prestige, tapping into the universe's abundance, getting rid of those things that do not support your wellbeing

Rune Yoga Practices: becoming aware of energy, honing sensory awareness, growing personal gifts and skills, gaining knowledge, connecting with ancestral memories

Associations: moveable wealth (cattle give milk, cheese, cream, butter, meat, leather, fertile manure, prestige, security), fertility, primal fire, productivity, spiritual and artistic creativity, creative fire, abundance, gain, plenty, gold, money, comfort, generosity, self-worth, monetary exchange, personal value, self-esteem, prosperity, gold kennings, drawing in energy, generative energy, sustenance, expansion, uplifts, inspiration, power, motion, movement, social success, beginnings, affirming, recognizing personal gifts, luck, Hamingja, possessions, exchange, emerging bounty, outward flow and expression, synergy, Life Force, financial strength and prosperity, calling/praying with an outpouring of energy, realized success, health, physical fulfillment, abundance, stocks and bonds, primal movement of energy, reinventing self, nourishment, fortune, financial strength, creation, circulation, abundance within new beginning, remembering, overflowing energy

Adverse Associations: blocks preventing abundance, disconnected from self, energetic blocks, greed, selfishness, insatiability, poverty, lack, spiritual poverty, extreme materialism, unhealthy, material loss, depleting resources, never being fulfilled, needy, inhibitions, grief, loss, bad trip, atrophy, discord, depleted, things falling apart, abundance disappearing, failure, health problems, poverty, unrequited, bad luck, debt, envy, possessiveness, hoarding. negative and depleting thought patterns

URUZ

Pronunciation: ooo-rooz
Sound: *u (true)*
Meaning: aurochs, slag, drizzle
Number: 1:2/2
Poems:

Old English
> Aurochs are fierce and high-horned
> with which they gore; a fierce fighter
> who bravely treads the moors.

Norwegian
> Slag is from bad iron;
> reindeer often run on hard snow.

Icelandic
> Drizzle is the weeping of clouds,
> and harvest's blight;
> an object hated by herdsman.

Ideograms: aurochs, drizzle
Visualization: aurochs standing in drizzle
Divinities: Eir, Sunna, Alateivia, Thor, Ullr, Vanir, Mother Earth, Urðr
Eddas, Sagas, and Stories: stories of men testing their strength and courage against wild aurochs, Thor and the giant's herd, the deluding of Gylfi, Urðr's Well; Ynglinga Saga Ch. 26
Healing: restoring health and vitality, muscular system, cervix and liver issues, strengthening immunity
Directions: southwest, north

Colors: red, greenish brown, orange, golden orange, light green, green, dark green
Elements: earth, water, ether
Natural Forces: earthquakes, drizzle
Plants: basil, green tea, nasturtium, sphagnum moss, Icelandic Moss
Trees: sycamore, maple, birch, oak
Incense: wintergreen
Gemstones: tiger's eye, jasper, carnelian, granite, nephrite, jade, carbuncle, emerald, green tourmaline, green beryl
Metal: iron slag
Living Creatures: aurochs, bull, ox, bison
Festival: August Eve
Day: Tuesday
Time of Day: 14:00, 1:30 PM – 2:30 PM
Time of Year: January 13 – February 3rd, July 14th – July 29th
Moon Phase: 1st quarter
Astrology: Mars, Taurus, Virgo, Capricorn, Sagittarius, Sun, Uranus, Leo
Tarot: High Priestess, Strength
Sacred Objects: Thor's belt (Megingjörð), Goddess' Girdle, drinking horn
Hall: Breiðablik
Nine Worlds: Hel
Zone: Inner Earth Space
Magical Beings: dwarves
Hávamál's Rune Poem (Ljóðatal): 147
Magical and Meditative Practices: drawing life force from the earth, inviting courage and strength, forgiving the self, letting go of guilt and blame, increasing vitality, strengthening virility, enhancing strength, removing doubt, inviting certainty, creating change and movement, strengthening the will, healing, making tangible, empowering, strengthening intuition, aligning and tapping into Earth's energies, strengthening OD, knowing the world through self, recognizing true self, touching in with primordial energies, discovering hidden patterns, creating patterns, shaping your reality with intention and will, inviting

fortunate circumstances, gaining knowledge and understanding of the self, magical understanding, getting rid of unwanted forces

Rune Yoga Practices: rooting and grounding energy, tapping into Earth's energy, building core strength, nine points of the foot, being fully in the moment

Associations: physical power, primal ground, primal forming force, roots of the World Tree, a challenge, trial, rite of passage, patterning force, tested, pushed to one's edge, personal growth, contest, test of strength, raw power, courage, renown, achievement, vigor, vitality, strong health, taking advantage of the moment, unconscious shaping energies, solidification, purification, patterning, reshaping, willpower, unconscious life-force, untamable, simplicity, grounding, centering, strength, stamina, endurance, rooted, rejuvenate, initiation, encouraging being fully present in the moment, galvanizing, sexual force, untamed force, to be and become, ordering principle, cosmic seed, self-formation, wisdom and lore, tenacity, luck, knowledge, understanding, ruling the land, healing, life-force, archetypes, potential, determination, ability to overcome, manifestation, persistence, structure

Adverse Associations: adversity, hostile forces, harshness, opposition, overwhelmed, difficulty, fear, losing, loss of strength, impotent, ignorance, illusion, controlled by sexual forces, weakness, obsession, misdirect forces, inconstancy, sickness, ignorance, missed opportunities, weak willpower, overcome by great forces, violence, reckless, uncontrollable energies, ungrounded, not belonging, loss of energy, guilt

THURISAZ

Pronunciation: thur-ee-sahz
Sound: _th_ (_thorn_ or _thunder_)
Meaning: giant, thorn, Thor's Hammer (Mjölnir)
Number: 1:3/3
Poems:

Old English
>Thorns are extremely sharp,
>painful to grasp
>and excessively severe to rest among.

Norwegian
>Thurs causes women's sickness;
>few are cheerful at misfortune.

Icelandic
>Giant is the torment of women,
>and the dweller of rocky vales
>and husband of Varthruna (warding Rune).

Ideograms: thorn, Mjölnir
Visualizations: bleeding from grabbing onto thorn bush, Thor wielding Mjölnir
Divinities: Thor, Loki, Farbauti, Ase, Thrud
Eddas, Sagas, and Stories: Hrungnir, Thor and the Frost Giants, Skírnir and Gerðr, Óðinn's sleep thorn (svefnþorn) in the _Volsungs Saga_ and a spell in the Huld Manuscript, Sleeping Beauty, Queen Ragnhild's Dream of a thorn _Saga Halfdan the Black_ Ch. 6
Kenning: Valkrie's Thorn (sword)

Healing: heart, menstrual difficulties, wounds caused by piercing, issues with bloodborne pathogens
Directions: southwest, south
Colors: purple, red, blood red, steel blue, violet, pure green
Elements: fire, air
Plants: spikenard, houseleek, thistle, bramble, black berry
Trees: blackthorn, hawthorn, oak, pine
Incense: dragon's blood
Gemstones: agate, bloodstone, red jasper, hematite, terminated crystal, jasper, garnet, carnelian, comets, tiger's eye, iron, broken glass, obsidian, sapphire, beryl, jacinth
Metal: iron
Living Creatures: snake, goat, cuckoo, scorpion, ram, wasp, hornet
Festival: August Eve
Day: Saturday
Time of Day: 15:00, 2:30 PM – 3:30 PM
Time of Year: February 4th – February 25th, July 29th – August 13th
Moon Phase: disseminating
Astrology: Saturn, Jupiter, Gemini, Libra, Aries, Mars, Scorpio
Tarot: Empress, Emperor, Justice
Natural Forces: electricity, thunder
Sacred Objects: thorn, knife, Mjölnir, Megingjörð, Járngreipr
Hall: Valaskjalf (shelf of the slain)
Nine Worlds: Miðgarðr
Zone: Jötunheimr
Magical Beings: giants, dragons
Hávamál's Rune Poem (Ljóðatal): 148
Magical and Meditative Practices: setting boundaries, protecting land, spells for strength and courage, dispel sickness, breaking up negativities, blasting away negative energies/beings, breaking down blocks, stagnation, and resistance, protection from being stabbed, directing energy, perceiving life's cycles, defense, destroying obstacles, awakening the will, love magic, cursing, destroying, warding, causing ill luck, preventing someone from waking up, piercing mental

cloudiness, confronting fears and unwanted habits, clearing entropy and energetic blockages, arousing sexual desire, overcoming negative patterns, bringing hidden things to light

Rite: Laying hammer in bride's lap

Rune Yoga Practices: honing the focus, starting to control energy by directing it, building willpower, recognizing and addressing with energetic triggers, destroying unwanted energies

Associations: directing raw power and energy, brute force, breaking down shields and barriers, awakener, clearing obstacles, honing and focusing energy, sexual power, powerful striking force, intensity, piercing reflection, thorny protection, willpower, power over life, dowsing, od-magnetic transfer, applied and controlled power, cosmic force of defense, instinctual will, assimilating and directing two streams of energy towards one thing, impregnating with energy, focusing thoughts, social forces, breakthrough, piercing, courage and strength, self-empowerment, reactive impulse

Adverse Associations: abrupt change, threat, danger, powerful disruption, pain, upset, painful experience, misfortune, thorny situations and relationships, disorder, lack of security, hostile forces, large, chaotic, and powerful opposition, being persecuted, blocked, unfair, upsetting order, inviting chaos, menstrual issues, clinging to things that cause pain, rushing forth, destructive forces, overwhelmed, negative energies, confusing, pierced, harmed, barren, either an ongoing pain or a devastating destructive force, aggression, destructive anger, violence, explosive, hurtful, triggering, repressed drives, compulsiveness, agitated situations, unconscious drives, dark magic, deception, damage, illness, accident, injury, unprotected, thinking negatively about others, betrayal, strife, sudden attack, war, wounds, depleting obsessions, lust, conflict, disputes, trouble, chaos, violent storms

ANSUZ

Pronunciation: awn-sooz
Sound: a (*all or art*)
Meaning: god, Óðinn
Number: 1:4/4
Poems:

Old English
> The mouth is the source of the word,
> bringing wisdom and council to the wise;
> hope and blessings to all.

Norwegian
> An estuary is the way for most farings,
> as the sheath is the way for swords.

Icelandic
> Odin is the ancient creator,
> and Asgard's chieftain,
> Valhalla's leader.

Ideogram: Óðinn's cloak blowing behind
Visualization: Óðinn's cloak blowing behind him
Divinities: Óðinn, Bird Goddess, Freya wearing falcon wings, Ásynjur
Eddas, Sagas, and Stories: Óðinn's origination story, creation, and breathing life into humans, (Sigdrifumál, 13-14), Óðinn stabbing sword into tree (*Volsung Sage* Ch.3), Óðrœrir (Hávamál 107 and Skáldskaparmál 5)
Healing: throat, respiratory system, emotional traumas affecting expression

Color: dark blue
Element: air
Natural Force: wind
Fungi: hallucinogenic
Plants: mistletoe, fennel, morning glory
Trees: ash, hazel
Gemstones: lapis lazuli, calcite, sapphire, jade, fluorite, aquamarine, labradorite, Herkimer diamond, emerald, sodalite
Living Creatures: raven, wolves, adders, horse, hawk
Festival: Yule
Day: Wednesday
Time of Day: 3:30 PM – 4:30 PM
Time of Year: August 13th – 29th
Moon Phase: gibbous
Astrology: Jupiter, Mercury, Pluto
Tarot: Hierophant, Death
Nine Worlds: Álfheim
Zone: Super Cosmic Space
Sacred Objects: runes, cloak, spear, feather
Magical Beings: woodwoses, woodwives
Hávamál's Rune Poem (Ljóðatal): 149
Magical and Meditative Practices: galdr, connecting with elemental forces, honing mental skills, tapping into inner knowledge, wisdom, and inspiration, influencing others with speech, enhancing ability to listen and understand, stopping the tongue of others, transformation, increasing clairvoyant powers, magical word, honing power of verbal influence, tapping into creative wisdom, experiencing ecstasy and divine connection, hypnotic speech, incantations, spells, re-writing personal story, death mysteries, touching the hearts of others, becoming the mouth of the divine, divination and prophesy, increasing magical powers, dispelling confusion, undoing tongue fetters and making people speak the truth, harnessing unconscious forces and emotions

Rune Yoga: controlling speech and thought, improving communication and listening skills, working with the breath, tapping into inspirations and insights, using the breath to increase energetic movement, clearing energetic blocks with focused breath and relaxation

Associations: wisdom, self-expression, inspiration, understanding, chanting, shapeshifting, wizardry, incantations, divination, transformations, rebirth, consciousness, intelligence, order, reason, ecstasy, opening, artistic inspiration and expression, wit over strength, integrating wisdom, spirit breath, galdr, thought, magnetic speech, mesmerize, channeling, finding voice, purifying, cleansing, clearing mental blocks, expanding consciousness, deepening awareness, binding and unbinding, speech, unfettering, transcending emotions, receiving messages, signals, signs, and answers, exploring the mysteries, education, self-awareness, divine source, discernment, inventive, ancestral power, reception, numinous knowledge, receiving, transmitting, communicating, releasing, seeking, cunning and mental agility, learning, Life-Breath, dreams, listening and paying attention, imparting information and knowledge, discovering and expressing personal truths, revelations, animating force

Adverse Associations: miscommunication, misinformation, misunderstanding, trickery, lies, falsity, deception, delusions, manipulation, boredom, gibberish, false knowledge, bad advice, mental manipulation, gossip, inability to express oneself, winded, mental fogginess, word salad or highly pressurized speech

RAIDO

Pronunciation: rye-do or rye-tho
Sound: *r* (*riding*)
Meaning: riding, carriage, road
Number: 1:5/5
Poems:

Old English
> Riding is easy for heroes inside a hall;
> yet strenuous to sit upon a powerful horse
> and ride for many miles.

Norwegian
> Riding is said to be the worst for horses;
> Reginn forged the best sword.

Icelandic
> Riding is a rider's joy,
> a swift journey
> and a horse's toil.

Ideograms: angled view of leg while riding a horse, wheel under carriage, sideview of someone holding reins of horse
Visualization: horse with rider going down path or across open field
Divinities: Gná, Loki, Thor, Nerthus, Forseti, Baldr
Eddas, Sagas, and Stories: Shinfaxi/Hrimfaxi, Regin sword-craft (*Volsung Saga* Ch.15), Óðinn's horse Sleipnir, Thor's carriage, Ing's story, example of horse toiling (*Hrafnkel Saga* Ch.5)
Healing: legs, circulatory system

Direction: south
Colors: red, yellowish white, pink, flame red, orange, green
Elements: fire, air
Plants: snapdragon, mugwort
Trees: holly, oak
Gemstones: moss agate, iolite, aventurine, ruby, sugilite, meteorite, turquoise, topaz, Jacinth, chrysoprase, lapis lazuli, carnelian
Living Creatures: horse, robin, hawk
Holy Tide: Ostara
Time of Year: August 29th – September 13th
Time of Day: 4:30 PM – 5:30 PM
Moon Phase: North Node
Astrology: Mercury, Leo, Virgo, Sun, Jupiter, Sagittarius
Tarot: High Priestess, Hierophant, Chariot
Nine Worlds: Álfheim
Zone: Cosmic Space
Sacred Objects: wagon, wheel, vehicle, sun
Magical Being: Reginn
Hávamál's Rune Poem (Ljóðatal): 150
Magical and Meditative Practices: aligning with the universal order, finding the proper direction, protection while traveling over land, moving energies, awakens higher centers of consciousness, strengthens magical skills, touching in with your inner truth and voice, gaining youthful vigor, strengthens and accelerates ritual outcomes, raising energy and consciousness in a balanced way, obtaining balance and justice, astral travel, find lost things and people, finding fruitful paths, can cause others to feel jittery and restless
Rune Yoga: circulating the body's energy, walking your talk, movement, dance, defining your path and moving towards it, syncing breath with movement, walking meditation
Associations: riding, doing something that invites pleasure but not without effort, the power that keeps people moving/acting, journey of life, expanding horizons, understanding and experiencing life, importance of movement and having life

experiences and asking questions like, "What am I doing? Where am I going?," movement, momentum, journey, travel, adventure, rhythm, motion, fluid and gracefulness, questing, seeking, channeling and moving energy, consciously traveling a path that works with both physical and spiritual planes, taking advantage of opportunities, overcoming obstacles, moving from one state to another, orderliness, advising and giving council, social boundaries, faring, proper timing, bring about social harmony, right action, timing and order, choosing one's path and how to walk it, controlling the passions, harnessing the will, personal journey, taking charge, being in control, counsel, right, freedom, moral responsibility, taking responsibility for decisions and actions, fully utilizing all that is within one's power and abilities, communication, union, reunion, attunement, reaching out to greater external forces, removing resistance, self-healing, unobstructed union, regulate excesses, trust in one's process, cut away illusions, find one's inner strength, undertake journey, clarifying, sifting, teaching, judging, cosmic rhythm, spiral development, physical cycles, hero, law, integrity, cycles of nature and celestial paths, organized religion, path back to balance and wholeness, good advice and judgment, ritual, cause and effect, good advice, measurement of time, social boundaries of time and space, living the story you are telling, circular forces, universal cycles, seeress, connecting with the pattern, dancing, trance work, inner journey

Adverse Associations: having a hard time/journey, going in circles, not getting anywhere, lack of movement or rhythm, failed attempts, fruitless movement, going astray, wasting energy, injustice, lawlessness, arbitrary, violence, disharmony, crisis, rigidity, stasis, irrationality, stagnation, failed travels, losing contact, unexpected arrival, forced movement

KENAZ

Pronunciation: kch-nawz or ka-nah
Sound: *k* (*candle*)
Meaning: torch, ulcer
Number: 1:6/6
Poems:

Old English
> A torch is known by its flame,
> illuminating and bright;
> often seen inside where nobles sit at ease.

Norwegian
> Ulcer is the curse of children;
> death/grief turns us pale.

Icelandic
> Ulcer is the bane of children
> and a scourge,
> a place of rotting flesh.

Ideogram: light spreading out from source
Visualization: torch illuminating the dark
Divinities: Heimdall, Óðinn, Saga, Sif, Freya, Three Norns
Eddas, Sagas, and Stories: Black Surt, Hávamál 2, 57, & 151, Grimnismal, Song of Rig, Egil loses his son Gunnar to fever (Egil's Saga Ch.79 verse 20), torches used to set fire to killed Thjazi (Skáldskaparmál 1)
Healing: digestion, fevers, oozing wounds
Direction: east
Colors: orange, amber, light red, gold

Element: fire
Plants: maidenhair fern, broom, cowslip, tobacco, gorse, wild rose
Trees: pine, spruce, bilberry, hazel
Incense: frankincense
Gemstones: topaz, citrine, tiger's eye, beryl, agate, bloodstone, flint, smoky quartz, fire opal, amber
Metal: flint and steel
Living Creatures: lynx, falcon, cat, lion, hawk, bobcat, peacock
Time of Day: 5:30 PM – 6:30 PM
Time of Year: April 13th – May 5th, September 13th – September 28th
Moon Phase: new, 3rd quarter
Astrology: Mars, Sun, Venus, Mercury
Tarot: Lovers, Chariot, High Priestess
Nine Worlds: Miðgarðr
Zone: Wave Space
Sacred Object: torch, candle, fire necklace, Brísingamen
Magical Beings: fire dwarves, fire giants, elf-cats, dragons, wyrms, phoenix
Hávamál's Rune Poem (Ljóðatal): 151
Magical and Meditative Practices: connect with fire, expelling darkness and ignorance, shining light on issues, protection, transformation, inner guidance, awakening insight and creativity, alchemy, transformation, purification, utilization of sexual energies, opening, clarity, shining light upon issues, banishing negativities and imbalances, illuminating, tapping into inspiration, increasing physical and mental wellbeing, increasing courage and strength, letting go, de-cluttering, Seiðr-fire, spiritual visions, burning away unwanted energies
Rune Yoga: burning away unwanted energies, building energy in core, transforming emotional energies using decoupling technique, increasing the body's capacity to work with more energy

Associations: torch, intense feelings over someone or thing, wisdom of the heart, burning desires, needing to learn how to kindle and retain flame, light, illumination, to perceive or become aware of, warmth, friendship, love, emotional fulfillment, creativity, enlightenment, inner light, unity, gathering together around a fire, direction and purpose, learning, gaining insight and knowledge, eroticism, guidance, burning away ignorance, shining a path, insights, realizations, conscious knowing, what inspires and makes you passionate, inner light, alchemical fire, hollowing, creative energy, memory, record-keeping, will, divine spark within, seeing through illusions and facades, clarity, personal talents, nobility, kindship, hearth and home, protection, crucible, purification, transformation, sexuality, health and vigor, emotional relationships, authority, consciousness, intellect, knowing, able to, cunning, art, confidence, storytelling, intuition, inspiration, enthusiasm, renewal, free to receive, seriousness, concentration, beginning work, time to come into the light, germination, light generator, drive and desire, chemical reactions, passion, hedonism, controlled fire, forge, cremation, transformative force, lust, sexual energy, cunning, scientific method, shines light on path/things, bringing things to light, birthing force, new relationship, time for conception, quickening

Adverse Associations: destructive fire, passions, and desires, burning, war, health issues, fever, ulcer, being ravaged by the fire, hasty, all-consuming, degenerative, not skilled, overthrown, disconnection, disease, decay, dissolution, inability, lack of creativity, coldness, ignorance, fever, lacking knowledge, insight, and understanding, ulcers, sores

GEBO

Pronunciation: geh-bow
Sound: *g* (*gift*)
Meaning: gift
Number: 1:7/7
Poem:

Old English
> Giving invites honor and grace of men,
> an adornment and support of dignity,
> while offering sustenance to those in poverty.

Ideograms: two people creating the "X" shape by shaking with both hands, or four people connecting one of their hands together
Visualization: two people exchanging gifts
Divinities: Gefion, Gefn, Vanir, Oðinn in giving his eye, giving himself to himself, and giving people the knowledge of the Runes and poetic tongue, Oski, Ygg, Thor, Freya
Eddas, Sagas, and Stories: (Hávamál 39, 41-42, 46, 48, 144, 164), Oðinn's gifts to people (form, breath, consciousness, inspiration, poetic skill, and Runes), (*Germania,* 21), Sigrdrifa
Healing: strengthening procreative power, respiration, clears poison, integumentary system, homeostasis
Direction: crossroads
Colors: emerald green, golden yellow, setting sun red, black, deep blue
Elements: air, earth
Plant: heartsease
Trees: ash, elm, yew, apple
Incense: patchouli, X

Gemstones: chiastolite, sugilite, staurolite, sapphire, emerald, jade, opal, rhodochrosite, malachite, jade
Living Creatures: sow, hen, goat, bee, dolphin, whale, eagle, bear
Festival: Yule
Time of Day: 6:30 PM – 7:30 PM
Time of Year: September 28th – October 13th
Moon Phase: full
Astrology: Venus, Virgo, Cancer, Pisces
Tarot: Moon, Lovers
Sacred Object: gifts
Nine Worlds: Miðgarðr
Zone: Wave Space
Magical Beings: sea-elves
Hávamál's Rune Poem (Ljóðatal): 164
Magical and Meditative Practices: balancing energies, inviting generosity and reciprocation, creating and severing bonds, healing, removing curses, sexual enchantments, binding, harmonizing relationships, cosmic consciousness, enhancing electro-magnetic currents, sex magic, mystical union, harmony between polarities, drawing what is needed for balance
Rune Yoga: balancing and harmonizing energies, centering, finding balance on all planes of experience, giving gifts
Associations: gift, exchange on all levels, generosity, sexual relations, giving and receiving, inner-connection, offerings, aid, assistance, charity, kindness, internal and external balance, energetic marriage, self-sacrifice for higher purposes, union, partnerships, oaths, contracts, growth, honoring and using personal gifts, kinetic balance, great effort to keep balance, exchange, compensation, agreements, reciprocation, settlements, boundary marker, integration, mutual partnership, what invites happiness, earth, reception, joining together, carrying, getting along, compassion, empathy, uniting, creating and strengthening bonds, unification, constant formulation and creation, marriage of two-selves, oneness, hospitality, reward, warm feelings and love, openness, sharing, trust in life,

connection between humans and the divine, hostage exchange, giving and receiving, recompense, trade, altruism, honor, gratitude, mark for treasure

Adverse Associations: non-reversible, extravagance, excessiveness, greed, money problems, selfishness, hoarding, imbalance, misdirected, disturbed, barren earth, disconnected, loneliness, dependence, over-sacrifice, excessive giving, taker

Standing in Gebo,
two energies cross paths:
touching,
connecting,
exchanging,
giving thanks.

Life is a gift,
don't waste it.

WUNJO

Pronunciation: woon-yo
Sound: *w* (*wind*)
Meaning: joy, victory flag, weathervane
Number: 1:8/8
Poem:

Old English
> Joy for those who know little woe, pain, or sorrow,
> blessed are they with prosperity and happiness,
> content within their strong hold.

Ideograms: banner, weathervane
Visualization: a joyful community gathered together to celebrate life
Divinities: Freyr, Freya, Vanir, Óðinn, Frigga, Vali, Ullr, Nerthus
Eddas, Sagas, and Stories: Hávamál 47 and 55, Sigdrifumál 6, Voluspá 61
Healing: mouth, lungs, endocrine system
Direction: wherever the wind blows
Colors: purple, green, yellow, light blue
Elements: air, earth
Fungi: fly agaric
Plants: pinkish lavender, ivy, flax, love-in-a-mist, larkspur, marigold, chamomile
Trees: ash, chestnut, lime
Incense: chamomile
Gemstones: kunzite, lepidolite, topaz, rose quartz, diamond, amber, quartz

Living Creatures: boar, swan, hound, stag, bee, horse, butterfly
Celebrations/Festivals: Minnisveig (curative drink for memory) and Sumbel (drinking ritual)
Time of Day: 7:30 PM – 8:30 PM
Time of Year: October 13th – October 28th
Moon Phase: gibbous
Astrology: Venus, Saturn, Leo
Tarot: Strength, Sun
Sacred Objects: spindle, spear, wedding ring, drinking horn, tribal flag
Magical Beings: elves
Magical and Meditative Practices: inviting success and peace, healing relationships, bringing likeminded people together, inviting tranquility and trust, creating positive bonds, clouding and mesmerizing minds, enslaving others through their desires, connecting different forces and energies together, touching in with joy and love, embracing positive emotions and thoughts, manifesting wishes, inviting happiness and contentment
Rune Yoga: experiencing spontaneous and lasting moments of joy, being fully present in the moment, learning to let go and flow with the energy, naked awareness
Associations: joy, pleasure, bliss, fulfillment, prosperity, growth, blessings, gain, plentifulness, wishing, buoyancy, happiness, favorable, deepening connections, gain, mutual support, pleasure through human interactions, abundance, ecstasy, success, good news and movement, emotional/mental/social healing, joy and connection in relationships (family, sexual, social), conscious union with divine. crown chakra, connecting with higher/divine self, recognizing and honoring one's self worth, recognizing the divine within all things, perfection, drive towards perfection, wish fulfillment, wonder, kinship, delight, accomplishments, enjoyment, manifestation of true will, relaxing and enjoying life, peaceful, winning, to win, light, come into one's own, freely

receiving the blessings of life, rejoicing, new energy and clarity, restoration, fruition, joy-filled laughter, harmony in relationships, like-minded/resonating, transcendental happiness, attraction, harmonious existence, binding different forces together, social harmony, fellowship, transformational substance, fellowship,

promoting goodwill, in the flow, realizing one's happiness, contentment, satisfaction, positive thinking and outlook, gladness, elevating one's thoughts, nearing fulfillment and completion, friendships, belonging, wellbeing, sharing in joy, emotional satisfaction, intrinsic rewards, everything going one's way, bonding, uplifting, effortlessness, found one's self, being fully present, wisdom gained through experience, fullness of life

Adverse Associations: unhappy, discontent, joyless, blocked energy and happiness, negativity, superficial/empty happiness, miserable, loneliness, sorrow, strife, alienation, not getting what you want, unfulfilled, bad timing, disappointment, betrayal, things not flowing, lacking joy and love, not seeing the blessings in life

HAGALAZ

Pronunciation: ha-ga-laz
Sound: h (*holy* or *hail*)
Meaning: hail
Number: 2:1/9
Poems:

Old English
Hail is the whitest of grains,
it whirls down from the skies above;
tossed by the winds before it turns into water.

Norwegian
Hail is coldest of grains,
Odin shaped the world with Ymir's body.

Icelandic
Hail is a cold grain
and a driving sleet
and the bane of snakes.

Ideogram: ice crystal
Visualization: hail falling to the ground and melting
Divinities: Urd, Holda, Hella, Heimdall, Gandreið, Þorgerðr and Irpa, Hella, Ancestors, Frigga, Ymir, Valkyries
Eddas and Sagas: Þorgerðr and Irpa (Jómsvíkinga saga, 21), Kari's Song in Njal's Saga, Göngu-Hrólfs Saga ch.28, Saga of Óláfs Tryggvasonar ch. 41-42

Kennings: "cloud's stone" for hail from Jómsvíkingadrápa, 32; "Hailstorm" for battle from The Saga of the Sworn Brothers pgs. 34 & 41, "chisel of snow" for hail from Egil's Sage ch.58, vs.32, Hail stones from eyes (tears)

Healing: kidney, bladder, lumbar pain, infected wounds

Colors: light blue, blue, luminous indigo blue, light green with white and red stripes, orange, grey

Elements: water, ice, hail

Plants: mandrake, henbane, nightshade, Lily of the Valley, bryony, fern

Trees: elder, fir, birch, willow, yew, ash, oak

Gemstones: rock crystal, black goldstone, jet, quartz, moonstone, striped agate, onyx, carbuncle, blue sapphire

Living Creatures: goose, nightjar, hound, beaver, otter, black stork, lizard

Time of Day: 8:30 PM – 9:30 PM

Time of Year: May 6th – May 28th, October 28th – November 13th

Moon Phase: full, 3rd quarter

Astrology: Saturn, Libra, Sagittarius, Venus, Aquarius

Tarot: Chariot, World, Tower

Sacred Object: veil, mantle

Magical Beings: huldrafolk

Nine Worlds: Ásgarðr

Zone: Wave Space

Hávamál's Rune Poem (Ljóðatal): 152

Magical and Meditative Practices: protection against storms and chaos, facilitates shamanic journeying, overcoming obstacles, sending destruction, hexing, connecting with the forces of the Universe, crone magic, preserves home from fire, protect self from injustice, conscious awareness of the divine within and around your, invites spiritual forces and wisdom, enhances pineal gland function as well as the sympathetic and solar plexus, balancing power, destroying all patterns, boundary breaker, not getting caught up, trusting in your ability to deal with chaotic and destructive circumstances and experiences, transformation, shadow workings, confronting past destructive patterns, breaking patterns and habits

Rune Yoga: breaking up and clearing away energetic blocks and stagnation, getting rid of unwanted thoughts and energies, triggering change, dealing with chaotic and disruptive forces in life, starting to work with and harness subconscious forces that trip you up, connecting with greater forces outside of yourself

Associations: gets rid of stagnation and weaknesses, spiritual decent, hidden emotions, potentiality, becoming, protection, bringing down fevers, dark feminine power, personal unconsciousness, first winter Rune, knowing your role in the divine pattern, world builder, Tree of Life, World Tree, inventiveness, turning circle, eternal exchange, union of mind and body, androgyny, Mother Rune, blessed union of procreation, hedge, enclosure, hiding within self, World Rune, sense, sound, color, harmony, wisdom, whole self, freedom, liberation, change, controlled crisis, completion, inner harmony, union, radical change, transforming from one world to another, unexpected shift, transforming perspective, breaking up things, testing and trials, harsh form of healing and cleansing, unconscious realm

Adverse Associations: disruptive natural forces, elemental powers, hail, mindless destruction, unwanted and or painful change, things outside of your control, breaking away, events and energy out of our control, loss, damage, breakups, discontinuity, suffering and hardships, inner turmoil, self-sabotage, self-destruction, chaotic thoughts, hateful and hurtful thoughts, storm, death, chaos, disruption, shipwreck, catastrophe, crisis, stagnation, love of power, loss of prosperity, setback

NAUDIZ

Pronunciation: naw-deez or now-theez
Sound: *n (necessity)*
Meaning: need
Number: 2:2/10
Poems:

Old English
> Need constricts the heart,
> yet often becomes a source of help and healing
> if heeded before its arrival.

Norwegian
> Need makes for little choice;
> the naked freeze in the frost.

Icelandic
> Need is the bondmaid's hardships
> and a hard circumstance
> and toilsome work.

Ideogram: bow and drill
Visualization: rubbing together of the bow and drill to create fire through friction
Divinities: Skuld, Sigyn, Nott, Norns
Eddas, Sagas, and Stories: Oðinn grasping the Runes, Oðinn bound between two fires, Fenris' binding, Loki's binding, slaves, story of Fatling's sons in Hávamál 77, Sigdrifumál 8
Healing: infections, skin diseases
Direction: south
Colors: black, dark red, light yellow, dark purple

Element: fire
Plants: crocus, bistort
Trees: alder, beech, rowan
Incenses: eucalyptus, black pepper
Gemstones: flint, obsidian, jet, lava stone, onyx, amethyst, lapis lazuli, hematite
Living Creatures: dog, lynx
Time of Day: 9:30 PM to 10:30 PM
Time of Year: May29th – June 20th, November 13th – November 28th
Moon Phase: 3rd quarter
Astrology: Scorpio, Capricorn, Sagittarius, Saturn
Tarot: Justice, Devil, Fool
Sacred Objects: bow and drill, chain
Nine Worlds: Niflheim
Magical Beings: black dragon, dwarves, the giant Jökul (Flateyjarbók), Níðhöggr
Hávamál's Rune Poem (Ljóðatal): 153
Magical and Meditative Practices: knot magic, banishing, overcoming restrictions, binding, finding a way, creating fire, settling negative issues, relieving suffering and hardships, understanding karmic debt, opening hidden channels of heart and voice, building the willpower, fulfilling deeper needs, deep inspiration arising from effort, self-discipline, gaining strength during difficult times, cleansing fire, counter-spells, controlling emotions and mind, releasing negative thoughts and emotions, cutting away all things that deplete and weaken you, burning away stagnation, obstacles, and inhibitions
Rune Yoga: continuing to work with subconscious forces, recognizing and addressing needs, letting go of fears and unhealthy attachments, learning to invite those things you need, overcoming negativity, developing willpower, sex magic, recognizing needs in self and others, fulfilling deeper needs
Associations: need, necessity, acceptance, facing difficulties, what is needed for a thing to exist and thrive, what is needed to move on, guarding against greed and materialism, spirit within the material, things taking their own time, slowness, need for

patience, taboos, boundaries, testing and teaching through hardships, tapping into inner strength, destiny, threading fate, lawfulness, primal law, inevitable, transformation, divine justice, emerging cross, karma, reconciliation, defense, forced to face truth, making the most out of destiny, cause and effect, impetus for movement and action, sail spar, innovation, self-reliance, taking action, acting with knowledge and wisdom, overcoming suffering and need, seeking to achieve, trusting in the flow, preserving energy, knowing that you get what is needed for spiritual journey, sexuality, passion, desire, resilience, survival, tempering, depth, not taking things personal, paying off debts, restore balance, mend and heal, time for purification, finding contentment

Adverse Associations: extremity, fear, delay, constraint, limitation, oppression, affliction, decline, ill-health, negative and draining thoughts, beliefs, and habits, struggle, compulsions, hardship, difficulties, discomfort, distress, restrictive, shadowy aspect of self, lack of options/choices, debt, personal guilt, unacknowledged needs, fettering, resistance, friction, craving, compulsion, desperation, binding, self-limitations, restraint, dissatisfaction, destruction, denial, disaster, loss, emergency, sacrifice, entanglement, discontent, self-imposed trials and burdens, toil, drudgery, being worn down, atrophy, laxity, trouble, insecurities, old patterns, unrequited, needs not met, imbalance, suffering, sexual frustration, compulsiveness, obsessive thinking and worrying, poverty, obstacles

ISA

I

Pronunciation: ee-sah
Sound: *e (freeze)*
Meaning: ice
Number: 2:3/11
Poems:

Old English
Ice is cold and slippery;
fair to behold that frost covered floor,
it's jewel like and glistering.

Norwegian
Ice we call a broad bridge;
the blind need to be led.

Icelandic
Ice is a river's bark
and a wave's thatch
and doomed men's undoing.

Ideogram: icicle
Visualization: frozen lake, icicle
Divinities: Verðandi, Skaði, Rindr
Eddas, Sagas, and Stories: Niflheim's part in creation, Skaði's marriage to Njórd, Auvandill's Toe (Skáldskaparmál)
Kennings: water's roof-shingle (anonymous poem from King Sagas), channel-sky (anonymous poem from King Sagas)
Healing: spine, liver, nervous disorders, paralysis, sensation loss, skeletal system
Colors: white, light blue, violet, grey, black

Elements: ice, water
Plants: heliotrope, sweet pea, Solomon seal, and sorcerer's periwinkle, henbane
Trees: blackthorn, elder, ash, birch, pine, oak, spruce, willow, beech, maple, chestnut, fir, alder
Incense: lavender
Gemstones: Herkimer diamond, diamond, white calcite, opal, clear quartz, cat's eye, blue sapphire
Living Creatures: wolf, seal, polar bear, reindeer
Time of Day: 10:30 PM – 11:30 PM
Time of Year: June 21st – July 14th, November 28th – December 13th
Moon Phase: waning
Astrology: Jupiter, Capricorn, Aquarius, Pluto, Moon
Tarot: Hermit
Sacred Objects: arrow, spear, sleep thorn
Nine Worlds: Niflheim
Zone: Material Earth Space
Magical Beings: frost giants, rime thurses, trolls, unicorns
Hávamál's Rune Poem (Ljóðatal): 154
Magical and Meditative Practices: nithing pole, hindering, slowing, and stopping energies and actions, inviting stillness, grounding, quietude, and peace, binding, paralyzing, empowers self and spells, strengthens resilience and willpower, deepens self-awareness, power over self and others, drawing power from the depths of being, becoming holy antenna, condensing energies, solidifying inner vision, breaking up stagnation and old patterns, protecting by freezing energy
Rune Yoga: seeking stillness, finding internal calmness, shoring up energy, letting go of depleting and disrupting things, coming into the moment, gaining some control over subconscious plane, dealing with stagnation in life, self-control, honing concentration, resting in a passive aware state, solidifying what you want, awareness of subtle energies, experiencing deeper states of relaxation

Associations: preserving, patience, shielding, protecting, cooling things down, slowing things down, disrupting negative or destructive energies, being aware of energies once the ice breaks, stillness, quietude, contemplation, centeredness, standing your ground, personal boundaries, resistance, materialism, self-preservation, conservation, solidification of ego-identity, rest, being present with what is, self-consciousness, formulating, workers, will, power, ego, personality, creative power, World Axis, phallus, concentration, self-control, unity of being, gathering, attraction/gravity, bonding, ego-awareness, cosmic egg, moment before the big bang, identity, endothermic, last winter Runes, withdrawal, focus, forced rest, calming, stabilizing, reflection, condensing and crystallizing, winter, inner-balance, serenity

Adverse Associations: barren, self-centered, lost momentum, taking away warmth, sterility, coldness, emotionally frigid, crisis, poverty, indecision, fixation, unrequited, unyielding, separation, imprisoned, addiction, psychosis, atrophy, danger, slippery circumstances, stalled, freezing emotions and thoughts, bad tripping, stuck emotionally, socially, mentally, and so on, sluggish energy, creating stillness, inertia, unconscious patterns, rigid ego-self, unchanging, unmoving, stubbornness, stagnation, inability to act, standstill, blockages, entangled, impeded, powerless, blind, surrender, unwanted sacrifices, frozen energy and situations, out of touch, cut off, rigid, lazy, dull, stupidity, limitations, paralysis, depression, unfocused, unfulfilled, lacking, stasis, conformity, harshness, apathetic, intolerance

JERA

Pronunciation: yair-ah
Sound: *y (year or Yule)*
Meaning: harvest, year, fruitful part of the year
Number: 2:4/12
Poems:

Old English
> Harvest time brings joy;
> the gifts of the gods
> to the rich and the poor.

Norwegian
> Harvest is the profit of men;
> I say that Fróði was generous.

Icelandic
> Harvest is the profit of all
> and a good summer
> and a ripened field.

Ideograms: two scythes, scythe cutting grains
Visualizations: horn of plenty, seeing a bountiful harvest, people harvesting
Divinities: Freya, Freyr, Sif, Baldr, Hodur, Verðandi, Sunna
Eddas, Sagas, and Stories: Mysteries of Baldr, Sif's hair being cut by Loki (Skáldskaparmál 5), story of Freyr giving good harvests (Saga of the Ynglings 10)
Healing: digestion, immune system, integumentary system
Direction: north

Colors: red, green, silver gray, orange, yellow, light blue, black
Element: earth
Plants: corn, rosemary, wheat
Trees: oak, holly, yew, fir, ash
Incense: rosemary, bergamot
Gemstones: moss agate, carnelian, moonstone, emerald
Living Creatures: Yule boar, goose, ox, eagle
Time of Day: 23:30-00:30, 11:30 PM – 12:30 AM
Time of Year: July 15th – August 7th, December 13th – December 28th
Moon Phase: 1st quarter
Astrology: Mercury, Sagittarius, Cancer, Sun, Saturn, Uranus, Earth, Jupiter
Tarot: Wheel, Fool, Emperor
Sacred Objects: mill stone, scythe
Magical Beings: elves
Hávamál's Rune Poem (Ljóðatal): 155
Magical and Meditative Practices: improving circumstances, building energy, increasing harvest, influencing time, tapping into solar power, magical concentration, banishing, salvation, touching in with electrical forces, vitality, strong effect on solar plexus, embodying spiritual light, increasing fertility, inviting harmony, enlightenment, awareness of cycles, sowing the seeds you want in your life and nurturing them until they blossom and bear fruit, protecting harvest, inviting healthy and prosperous change, manifesting desired effect
Rune Yoga: taking responsibility for your choices in life, enjoying and giving thanks for the fruits of your labors while also recognizing and working with the larger patterns in your life, working with time, creating new patterns of fruitfulness, inviting empowering thoughts and behaviors, connecting with nature's cycles

Associations: eternal return, fertility, harvest, fertile season, year, beneficial outcomes, committed efforts, no quick result expected, complete cycle, cultivation, perseverance, natural movement/cycle of the universe, balance, abundance, time, circular movement, success, reaping what you sow, justice, developing, progressing, gardening and farming, circle, enclosed space or time, good spirits, completeness, ripe, fulfillment, plenty, winter survival, goal setting, purpose, inherent quality, achievements, wisdom, beauty, virtue, trust, honor, glory, light carrier, salvation, completion, clearing debts and karma, noble, harmony, Sun-being, healer, increase, harmonious relations, reward, peace, good timing, seasons, biorhythms, orbits, prosperity, creativity, growth, fruitfulness, turning, change, easy, joy, good things, hope, cycling opposites like day and night or winter/summer and spring/fall

Adverse Associations: malice, darkness, confusion, magical illusion. back tracking, repetition, bad timing, poverty, conflict, hunger, regression, depletion, desperation, broken cycle or tradition, unwanted consequences, unhealthy habits and patterns, fruitless, joyless, wasted talents or efforts

EIHWAZ

Pronunciation: ay-waz, ay-hahz, i-waz
Sound: *ay (w<u>ay</u>), a (v<u>at</u>), i (d<u>ie</u>)*
Meaning: yew tree
Number: 2:5/13
Poems:

Old English
    Yew is rough without,
    hard inside and deeply rooted;
    it's fire's keeper and a joy in the homeland.

Norwegian
    Yew is the greenest wood in winter;
    when it burns there's usually singeing.

Icelandic
    Yew is a bent bow
    and a brittle tool
    and arrow's lightning.

Ideogram: yew tree's branch and root
Visualizations: yew tree, bow
Divinities: Ullr, Fárbauti, Oðinn, Frigg, Skaði
Eddas, Sagas, and Stories: Yggdrasil, Óðinn hanging from tree for Runes
Kenning: Egil's weapon for "bow" (Hákonardrápa 2),
Healing: spine, urinary system
Direction: south
Colors: dark green, dark blue

Element: all
Plants: lilac, mandrake
Trees: yew, hemlock
Incense: benzoin
Gemstones: topaz, smoky quartz, turquoise
Living Creatures: spider, snake, raven, moth
Time of Day: 12:30 AM – 1:30 AM
Time of Year: December 28th – January 13th
Moon Phase: South Node, disseminating
Astrology: Jupiter, Mercury, Scorpio
Tarot: Hangman, Death
Sacred Objects: distaff, bow
Magical Beings: dises, dragons
Hávamál's Rune Poem (Ljóðatal): 161
Magical and Meditative Practices: life and death mysteries, magical endurance, protection, increasing personal power, developing spiritual endurance and will, past life experiences, communication with the dead, shamanic trance, finding lost things, causing death, gaining wisdom, traversing the worlds, protection against illusions, communicating between realms, letting go, astral travel, soul searching, cutting away the dead energy, connecting with ancestral wisdom, banishing unwanted energies
Rune Yoga: severing dead and unwanted energies and aspects of yourself, ending toxic and harmful relationships, trance work, experiencing deeper states of being, communicating between realms, extending consciousness beyond conceptualized self, aligning all aspects of the self together
Associations: death, immortality, hollow center, gateway, transition, threshold, grave, regeneration, defense, avoiding and preventing unbalancing and unwanted situations and energies from arising, allowing the energies to dissolve on their own, patience, waiting, foresight, think before acting, hunting, assertive, persistence, striving, testing, going for it, evolving, psychological suspension, will, idealism, strengthening, creating foundation, World Axis, carrying energies between opposites,

shamanic journeying, paradox, turning of events, upright and downturned Laguz (flowing up and down), politics, communication, system theory, enlightenment, initiation, life giving force, banishing. connecting the heavens, earth, and underworld together, transformation, clearing obstacles, examination, old self-giving way to the new, turning point of Rune sequence, authenticity, bouncing back

Adverse Associations: confusion, destruction, dissatisfaction, weakness, struggle, ordeals, hang-ups, death, sickness, withering away, darkness, uncertainty

PERTHO

Pronunciation: pear-throw
Sound: *p (possibilities)*
Meaning: unknown
Number: 2:6/14
Poem:

Old English
> Gaming invites play and laughter
> among the high-spirited sitting
> happily together in the mead hall.

Ideograms: dice cup, lot cup, drinking cup, female legs giving birth, mother's womb, volva
Visualizations: throwing dice from a gambling cup, mother giving birth, people playing games and hearing laughter
Divinities: Norns, Frigg, Nerthus, Mímir, Mother Goddess, Gefjun
Eddas, Sagas, and Stories: Völuspá 8 & 61, Svipsdagmál 16, Sigdrifumál 9, Morkinskinna 71, Konungs skuggsjá 24
Healing: breasts, female genitalia, birth, skeletal system
Direction: north
Colors: dark purple, red, white, black, silver
Element: water
Plants: chrysanthemum, aconite, monkshood, dandelion, daisy
Trees: yew, elder, beech, aspen, pear, elm, apple
Incense: yarrow, nutmeg, yew
Gemstones: aquamarine, onyx, meteorite, gold topaz
Living Creatures: owl, spider, frog, chameleon
Time of Day: 1:30 AM – 2:30 AM
Time of Year: January 13th – January 28th

Moon Phase: South Node
Astrology: Mars, Saturn, Uranus
Tarot: Wheel of Fortune
Sacred Objects: game pieces, tally staves, wells, volva
Magical Beings: phoenix
Magical and Meditative Practices: understanding Wyrd, unlocking ancestorial memories, increasing odds, calling upon luck, revealing secrets, divination, inviting luck, increasing fertility, knowledge of Örlög, Wyrd Workings, deeper self-knowledge, discovering the truth, seeing what other's don't want you to see, causing others to revel something, birth mysteries following Eihwaz's death mysteries, manipulating cause and effect, inviting favorable circumstances, strengthening guessing power
Rune Yoga: connecting with the different parts of your soul, defining who you want to be on all levels, increasing odds with energy, giving birth to new things which is always a gamble, revealing what is hidden
Associations: unknowable, inner transformative forces, active power behind destiny, consequences, free will vs environmental and circumstantial constraints, not easy, unexpected gains, flight of the eagle, deepest aspect of being, psychic death, letting go of everything, gathering and harmonizing scattered energies, memories, birth, space, hidden aspects, introspection, not everything is as it appears, outside sources for guidance, hidden things coming to light, second chance, finding something lost, secrets, sex, gambling, speculating, entrance to a closed space, group, or situation, problem solving, esoteric knowledge, synchronicity, initiation, inventive, unconventional, fate, working in accordance with primal laws, going with the flow, Uncertainty Principle, understanding the past in order to better shape the future, good omens, recognizing patterns, knowledge of Örlög, fellowship, joy, evolutionary change, personal luck, divination, choice, weaving, Goddess Wisdom, seeing into the past, present, and future, womb, prophecy, hidden information, change, unknown, new beginning, renewal, guessing, self-determination, fertility, revelations

Adverse Associations: addiction, stagnation, loneliness, malaise, insecurity, unwanted situation, birth troubles, sexual frustration, failure, bad toss of the dice or bad card hand, reproductive issues, uncertainty, unknown, stillborn, gambling problems, unconscious issues, tripping yourself up, unable to understand, wrong answers, unwanted secrets revealed, patterns and energies working against you, careless

ALGIZ

Pronunciation: al-geez
Sound: ʒ (*buzzing*)
Meaning: elk, elk sedge
Number: 2:7/15
Poem:

Old English
    Elk sedge dwells in fens
    and grows in water,
    wounding and staining with blood all who grasp it.

Ideograms: elk antlers, elk-sedge grass, antenna
Visualizations: standing elk, person standing with arms upraised and a Bifröst rainbow is seen past them
Divinities: Freya, Heimdall, Valkyries, Óðinn
Eddas, Sagas, and Stories: Ægishjálmr (Fáfnismál 16), Galdrabók, Volsungs 20
Healing: abdomen, male sexual organs, head stuff like headaches and sinus problems
Colors: bluish silver, grey, black, gold, silver, rainbow
Element: air
Plants: sedge, rush, angelica, marigold
Trees: rowan, elderberry, yew, lime, linden, spruce
Incenses: juniper, peppermint, rosemary
Gemstones: black tourmaline, topaz, bloodstone, amethyst, jasper
Metal: iron, steel
Living Creatures: swan, elk, raven, moose, stag
Time of Day: 2:30 AM – 3:30 AM

Time of Year: Nov 30th – Dec 21st, January 28th – February 12th
Moon Phase: full
Astrology: Cancer, Moon, Mars, Jupiter, Venus
Tarot: Tower, Moon
Sacred Objects: Gjallarhorn, Helm of Awe (Ægishjálmr), Valkyrie's swan garment, shield
Magical Beings: Valkyries (Swan Maidens)
Magical and Meditative Practices: protection, touching in with higher consciousness, warding, attracting divine energies, mastering of lower nature, listening to instincts, seeking truth and guidance, plant magic, connecting with the higher self, honing the senses, increasing life-force, connecting with inner divinity and sacredness
Rune Yoga: empowerment, shielding protection, tapping into the Earth's energies while opening to the celestial energies, connecting with fetch, wights, ancestors, and the Æsir and Vanir
Associations: magical protection, warding off unwanted energies, prepared, unseen forces watching over you, defense, shielded, temple, sanctuary, crow's foot, sedge, elk, control of emotions, transition, acceleration, stimulation, mindful, healthy, variable, changeable, waxing and waning, flexible, higher self, preserving, receiving, collecting, balance between inner and outer worlds, defense on all levels, good fortune, fortunate circumstances and influences, higher marriage, eternal, procreation, nature's law, relationship fulfillment, merging, love, divine connection, awakening, higher life, courage, passively protective, place of personal safety, high vibrational protection, radiating love, growth, sprouting, safe refuge
Adverse Associations: defenses are down, defenseless, internal battle, danger of attack, lack of protection, peril, bondage, egoism, chaos, falsehood, malice, perversion, reprehensible acts, bad influences, misunderstanding, confusion, insanity, denial, destruction, temptation, delusional, loss of divine link, feeling lost, alone, distant, health problems, weakness, vulnerabilities, out of touch, lacking intuition

SOWILO

Pronunciation: so-wee-lo
Sound: *s (sun)*
Meaning: sun, sun beam/ray
Number: 2:8/16
Poems:

Old English
> The sun brings hope
> to the seafarer's journey
> as they cross the sea and come to land.

Norwegian
> Sun is the light of the lands;
> I bow to holy judgment.

Icelandic
> Sun is the cloud's shield
> and a blazing ray
> and ice's destroyer.

Ideograms: lightning bolt, sun rays
Visualizations: sun, sunbeam
Divinities: Sunna/Sol, Thor, Baldr
Eddas, Sagas, and Stories: Mundilfari, Sigdrifumál 10, Alvismál 15-16, Grímnísmál 37-39
Sun Kennings: fair jewel of the high storm-house, flame of the clouds, fire of the sky, light-jewel, adorner of the earth
Healing: tendons, nervous system, heart, digestive system
Direction: south
Colors: golden-white, clear blue, white, silver, yellow

Element: fire
Plants: St. John's wort, mistletoe, daisy
Trees: yew, juniper, oak, bay
Incenses: juniper, sandalwood, amber, frankincense,
Gemstones: ruby, sunstone, jasper, carnelian, amethyst, citrine, topaz, amber, Icelandic spar
Living Creatures: hawk, bee, eagle, hare
Time of Day: 3:30 AM – 4:30 AM
Time of Year: August 8th – 30th, February 12th – February 27th
Moon Phase: full
Astrology: Sun, Aquarius, Gemini, Uranus, Neptune, Aries, Taurus
Tarot: Sun, Strength
Sacred Objects: chariot, solar wheel, Brísingamen
Nine Worlds: Muspellheim
Zone: Cosmic Space
Magical Beings: sun-wights
Hávamál's Rune Poem (Ljóðatal): 156
Magical and Meditative Practices: touching in with inner guidance, bringing light to the unknown, illuminating, healing, divination, inviting victory and success, overcoming obstacles, enhancing mental powers, inviting insight and wisdom, victory over lower self, protection from injustice, hatred, enemies, generating a strong force, recognizing inner divinity, breaking negative habits and patterns, inviting more joy and compassion in life
Rune Yoga: connecting with solar energies, deepening conscious experience, witness meditation, embodying the light, fully awakening the body's energy
Associations: wholeness, embodying the divine, higher self, divine spark, consciousness, enlightenment, brightness, prosperity, destroying darkness and ignorance, coming into your own, embodying your truth, dynamic connection between earth and heaven, life force, transformative will, self-victory, illumination, movement, lightning, kundalini, clarification, guiding principle, strength, energy, health, success, achievement, honor, connecting with the Sun (color, shape,

warmth, affect, season, heavenly relationship, et cetera), intention, self-worth, individuation, inner-self, healing, warmth, sun's energy, impulse towards self-realization and actualization, positivity, self-confidence, motivation, hope, harmony, victory, fertility, vigor, vitality, path to be followed, great power, recharging and regeneration, watch how you use energy, retain strength, build energy and move forward with focus and intention, salvation, mental contemplation, clarification, solution, liberation, way of the divine, electricity, chakras, magical will, light, soul, guidance, beacon, goals, path of ecstasy, understanding, insight, revelation, faith in outcomes, spiritual growth, triumph, guardian, might, endlessly moving, love

Adverse Associations: in the dark, ignorant, blinded, obsessive urges and desires, cold selfishness, burning bridges, improper means and exploitation, division, dissolution, fragmentation, infirmity, hopeless, lost, darkness, unhealthy goals, bad advice, dishonorable success, gullibility, loss of goals, blocked sun, conceit, unhealthy egotism, vanity

TIWAZ

Pronunciation: tea-waz
Sound: *t (Tyr)*
Meaning: Tyr
Number: 3:1/17
Poems:

Old English
> Tir is a guiding sign, traveling forth
> it never fails, is always true,
> keeping faith through night's gloom.

Norwegian
> Tyr is the one-handed among the Aesir;
> the smith is blowing often.

Icelandic
> Tyr is the one-hand god
> and the wolf's leavings
> and temple's protector.

Ideograms: sword, spear point, penis
Visualizations: spear tip, arrow point, balanced scale
Divinities: Týr, Forsetti, Mani
Eddas, Sagas, and Stories: Gylfaginning 25 & 34, Sigdrifumál 6
Tyr Kennings: one-handed god, god of battles, fosterer of the wolf, Fenrir's feeder, the god of the þing, Hymir's son, Garm's last meal

Healing: gout, rheumatism, hardening of arteries, hands and wrist, helping with balance and body regulation, strengthening immune system
Direction: north
Colors: crimson, reddish gray, gray blue, light red, purple, right red, brown, blood red
Element: air
Plants: red hot poker, monkshood, elderberry, sage, aconite
Trees: oak, elder, hazel
Incenses: thyme, lemongrass, verbena
Gemstones: coral, bloodstone, hematite, charoite, topaz, ruby
Metal: steel
Living Creatures: cockerel, rooster, wolf
Festival: presides over the Þing
Day: Tuesday (Tyr's Day)
Time of Day: 4:30 AM – 5:30 AM
Time of Year: August 31st – September 22nd, February 27th – March 14th
Moon Phase: dark moon
Astrology: North Star, Mars, Pisces, Libra, Sagittarius, Neptune
Tarot: Hangman, Justice, Wheel of Fortune
Sacred Objects: sword, Irminsul pillar, Frigg's spindle and distaff, spear
Zone: Wave Space
Nine Worlds: Miðgarðr
Magical Beings: Fenrir, Shining Ones
Hávamál's Rune Poem (Ljóðatal): 157
Magical and Meditative Practices: seeking spiritual enlightenment, bringing about justice, honing focus, overcoming trials, gaining honor, strengthening will, helping to maintain order, overcoming earthly materialism, overcoming fear of death, tapping into past lives, inviting prosperity, astral travel, seeking immortality, aligning physical and spiritual goals, increasing attractiveness, finding your way when lost, achieving victory against the odds, finding guidance, strengthening belief, magical oaths

Rune Yoga Practices: taking up a cause and being willing to fight for something greater than yourself, transmitting energy to others, defining the meaning and purpose of your life

Associations: directed and unwavering focus, warrior energy, unattached from outcomes, staying the course, being true to self, discernment, patience, active principle, urge for conquest, single-mindedness, timely, setting priorities, not being hasty, not wasting energy, competition, motivation, willpower, stamina, moral strength, fertility, increase, finding your path, law, contacts, oaths, social values, victory, justice, valor, courage, spiritual warrior, unbiased, authority, combined strength, fairness, inner strength, leadership, determination, strength in battles, honor, fame, respect, praise, legal manners, tree, sacrifice, resurrection, affirmation, origin, eternal change, regeneration, over life, self-sacrifice, growth, prosperity, testing, balance, spiritual discipline, overcoming difficulties, scientific method, impartial, discipline, logic, loyalty, rationality, analysis, nobility, peace keeping, structure, responsibility, inner guidance, spring, weaving, positive and directed natural order, honesty, fair, truth, guidance, navigation, fatherhood, stability, lawful, morality, duty, responsibility, authority, reliable, optimistic, bravery, daring, dedicated, tactical, legislative, negotiating, having a mission, fighting for what you believe in, oaths, world order, focusing on solutions, oaths

Adverse Associations: destruction, laceration, greed, perdition, mental paralysis, over analyzing, over sacrifice, imbalance, defeated, tyranny, injustice, strife, arguments, battling, separation, lost, unfocused, cowardice, lacking direction or purpose, unmotivated, dishonorable, dishonest, betrayal, fearful, selfishness, not taking responsibility, battling with self, judgmental, confrontation

BERKANA

Pronunciation: bear-ka-nah
Sound: *b (birth)*
Meaning: birch
Number: 3:2/18
Poems:

Old English
>   Birch is fruitless and yet bears shoots without seed,
>   its beautiful branches are laden with leaves
>   as its lofty crown touches the sky with ease.

Norwegian
>   Birch is the leaf-greenest of branches;
>   Loki had luck in deceit.

Icelandic
>   Birch is a leafy limb
>   and a little tree
>   and youthful wood.

Ideograms: two mountains, mother's breast, breast and belly of pregnant woman, fold the triangles together we get a diamond, which hints at the womb and a protective place
Visualizations: birch tree, breast and belly of pregnant mother
Eddas, Sagas, and Stories: used like a ladder in trance work (*Gods and Myths*, 192), Sigdrifumál 11,
Divinities: Bercha/Bertha, Laufey, Holda, Freya, Mother Earth, Nerthus, Hel, Frigga
Healing: birth and womb
Direction: east

Colors: white, green, light blue for day and light purple for night, red blue, dark blue, dark green
Element: earth
Plants: moonflower, lady's mantle
Trees: birch, fir
Incense: dill
Gemstones: moonstone, jet
Living Creatures: bear, pheasant, badger
Time of Day: 5:30 AM – 6:30 AM
Time of Year: September 23rd – October 15th, March 14th – March 30th
Moon Phase: crescent
Astrology: Moon, Jupiter, Aries, Scorpio, Mars, Virgo
Tarot: Death, Empress
Sacred Objects: besom, cradle
Nine Worlds: Jötunheimr
Zone: Wave Space
Magical Beings: skogsrå, wood elves
Hávamál's Rune Poem (Ljóðatal): 158
Magical and Meditative Practices: optimizing new beginnings, bringing things to a positive conclusion, protecting loved ones, developing magical and mystical abilities, soul-awakening, resolving entanglements, finding inner freedom, birth of higher mind, touching in with finer forces of nature, strengthen powers of secrecy; magical concealment, protection, bringing ideas to fruition, protecting pregnancy, increasing fertility, purifying, ritual blessings
Rune Yoga Practices: creating a plan to manifest your intentions, energy consolidation, connecting with the Earth and Mother, giving birth to new ideas and fruitful actions, honing intuition, self-care and love
Associations: birth, purification, fertility, inception, new phase, detoxification, favorable time for initiating projects, fruitful, regeneration, pregnancy, renewal, generative energy, sexual pleasures, healing, comfort., generation, conception, beginning, growth, rebirth, ripening, protecting abandoned children, rejuvenating, protective, nurturing, family life, origin, shelter,

revelation, uterus, deep inside the mountain, breasts, eternal life, budding, blooming, life, being, tender loving care, motherhood, biology and earth sciences, spring, mothers, procreation, concealment, hidden, passive receptor, conserving force, sanctuary, life changes, liberation, fruitful opportunity, nurturing energy, intuition, emotional healing

Adverse Associations: difficult in initiating projects, problem with plans, wrong time, poor conditions, careless, pregnancy issues, homeless, vulnerable, nude, negativity, deluded hopes, unfulfilled desires, outcast, miscarriage, inglorious death, blurred consciousness, deceit, sterility, stagnation, not loving or nurturing oneself, imprisoned, energy

EHWAZ

Pronunciation: eh-waz
Sound: *eh (led)*
Meaning: horse
Number: 3:3/19
Poem:

Old English
> Hoof-proud steeds before warriors brings joy to the nobles,
> as heroes and the wealthy on war-horses exchange words,
> solace is brought to the restless.

Ideograms: side view of a standing horse, horse's ears from rider's perspective
Visualization: riding a horse
Divinities: Freya, Freyr, Epona
Eddas, Sagas, and Stories: Árvakr and Alsvithr, Sleipnir and Svadilfari, King Eirik Bloodaxe cursed by Egil's nithing pole, Freyfaxi, Fylgia, Vǫlsa þáttr
Horse Kennings: saddle-beast, ship of the league
Healing: melancholy, gland inflammation and enlargement, arm and leg issues, respiratory system
Direction: west
Colors: red-orange, light yellow in day and greenish at night, white
Element: earth
Plants: forsythia, ragwort, ground sorrel
Trees: alder, oak, ash, aspen

Incense: grapefruit
Gemstones: Icelandic spar, malachite, turquoise, beryl, calcite, sapphire, agate, sardonyx
Living Creatures: horse
Time of Day: 6:30 AM – 7:30 AM
Time of Year: March 30th – April 14th
Moon Phase: 1st quarter
Astrology: Mercury, Leo, Gemini, Venus
Tarot: Star, Lovers
Sacred Objects: bridal and saddle, horse penis
Magical Beings: Freyfaxi, Sleipnir, horse-wights, night-mares
Hávamál's Rune Poem (Ljóðatal): 162
Magical and Meditative Practices: controlling emotional and instinctual energies, binding, inviting positive movements, helping things progress, astral travel, finding twin soul, dissolving lower passions, purification, creating pure thoughts, speeds things up, extending status and power, harmonizing body and mind, unifying, astral travel, travel between worlds, helps with communication, controlling feelings, nithing-pole, setting boundaries
Rune Yoga: manifesting your intentions, expanding consciousness, inspiring and motivating others, astral travel, overcoming inhibitions, blocks, stagnation, laziness, and inaction, making change happen
Associations: transportation, vehicle, mobility, travel, setting boundaries, need for movement and variety, fertility (preserving horse penis), change, marriage, eternity, forever, holy, equal, lifetime, life force, life span, increasing physical power, extending human reach over distances, helping with hunting and warfare, expansion of consciousness, increasing capacity, going in the right direction and doing the right things, solving problems, accomplishing will, overcoming obstacles, marriage, partnerships, adjusting to circumstances and situations, instinctive drives, sexuality, adaptability, subjectivity, anima, physical shifts, new homes, new attitudes, new life transitions, gradual development, steady progress, procreation, pure power of life, unity, harmony between two, sensuality, movement,

horse and rider are one, sensual pleasure while riding, mobility, stages in chemical and atomic reactions, unification of two or more energies towards one aim, empowering: teamwork, trust, loyalty, change for the better, journey, trusting and flowing with life's energies, extending access, gaining more power and reach, oscillation of movement, spiritualizing one's life, soul mate

Adverse Associations: restless, feeling stuck and stagnant, feeling constricted, unhappy marriage, unrequited love, disconnected, duplication, disharmony, mistrust, betrayal, too quick movement without ground or reflection

MANNAZ

Pronunciation: mah-naz
Sound: *m (man)*
Meaning: man (with general sense of human beings)
Number: 3:4/20
Poems:

Old English
    We are each other's mirth
    yet all must one day take their leave,
    for the gods allot by fate's decree:
    frail flesh must return to the earth and sea.

Norwegian
    Man is earth's increase;
    the hawk's grasp is great.

Icelandic
    Man is man's joy
    and earth's increase

Ideogram: two people embracing
Visualizations: seeing a loved one, being lost and then being found by someone, embracing someone with genuine love and goodwill
Divinities: Heimdall, Óðinn
Eddas, Sagas, and Stories: Ask and Embla, Rígsmál 46, Hávamál 47
Human Kennings: wealth-yearners, sons of the earth, collector of gold, shaker of shields (warrior), Ríg's offspring

Healing: injuries, nervous disorders, tendon pain, feet and ankle issues, circulatory issues
Colors: white, red, green, purple, blue, dark red, deep red
Element: air
Plants: foxglove, madder
Trees: ash, elm, holly, maple, alder
Incense: clove
Gemstones: garnet, amethyst, onyx, emerald, turquoise
Metal: gold
Living Creatures: humans, ram, wolf
Time of Day: 7:30 AM – 8:30 AM
Time of Year: November 8th – 29th, April 14th – April 29th
Moon Phase: full
Astrology: Saturn, South Node, Gemini, Sun, Moon, Jupiter, Aquarius, Pisces
Tarot: Devil, Magician
Sacred Objects: horn, ax, plough, mirror
Hávamál's Rune Poem (Ljóðatal): 160
Magical and Meditative Practices: building spiritual relationships, increasing powers of the intellect, cunning, and reason, improving concentration, clearing and focusing the mind, creating social harmony, protection from against hostile forces, mental protection, increasing spiritual energies, peace, strength, and health, awakening divine magic, sensing universal love, banishing threats, unifying with universe, balancing self., balancing body, mind, and spirit, connecting with personal Wyrd, experiencing wholeness, coming into our own, expanding consciousness, recognizing connection to Mother Earth, embodying whole self
Rune Yoga: living your truth, deepening self-awareness, increasing intelligence and wisdom, building positive and empowering relationships, self-control, seeking energetic empowerment

Associations: humans, kinship, society, human potential, human power and energy, human talents and gifts, human skills and abilities, self, willingness to change, modesty, time of growth and rectification, be fully present with what is, being clear and truthful with oneself, social structure, intellectual capabilities, mind, divide, senses, sensations, feelings, judge, intent, memory, interdependence, magical potential, human's condition, community, bravery, giving, human archetype, character, humanity, ascending, truth, divine magic, ego, blood brother, fellowship, bonding, conscious movement towards inner divinity, breath, spirit, soul, and body, awakening, working, governing, elevating, divine structure, intelligence, awareness, social order, divine influence, rationality, human wholeness and perfection. taking care of personal needs, inner being, people, friends and family, clarity, tolerance, humane, charity, creativity, forethought, nobility, culture, third-eye, assistance, teamwork, cooperation, ancestral memory, female wisdom, unity of body and mind, healing mind/body split, oneness, connection, social contract, balance between needs of self and other, fair trade, treating others with respect, human identity, function, and purpose, social relationships, clear thought, how we came to be and who we are, heredity, role in society, self-knowledge

Adverse Associations: insanity, madness, greed, depression, mortality, blindness, self-delusion, stupid, ignorant, mentally foggy or frazzled, slow witted, dishonesty, cruelty, bigotry, elitism, disconnected, classist, SPECIESISM, without human connection, inflated ego, selfish , arrogance, not living up to full potential, stubborn, irrational

LAGUZ

Pronunciation: lah-gooz
Sound: *l (leek or lake)*
Meaning: lake, leek
Number: 3:5/21
Poems:

Old English
> Water to people seems unending
> when they set sail on a heaving ship;
> the sea waves overwhelm them
> as the brine-stallion ignores its bridle.

Norwegian
> Water, as streams, fall from mountains;
> golden trinkets are costly things.

Icelandic
> Water is a bubbling stream
> and a wide kettle
> and the fishes land.

Ideograms: bent leek, water spigot
Visualization: ocean, rivers, reflective pond, a bed of leeks smiling at you in the snow
Divinities: Njörðr, Aegir, Ran, Mani, Baldr, Mother Holle
Eddas, Sagas, and Stories: Sea Runes in the Lay of Sigdrifa, Freyr's ship, Sigdrifumál 9 mentions spell to protect from poisoning, 1st Lae of Helgi 7, Óláfs Saga Helga mentions using leeks as a healing spell (*Heimskringla*, 52)

Healing: infections, skin diseases, healing emotional imbalances, urinary system, endocrine system
Direction: west
Colors: blue, pale blue-green, fire red for day and ruby for night, brown, green blue, deep green
Element: water
Plants: water lily, water cress, leek
Trees: willow, spruce, linden-tree
Incense: jasmine, myrrh
Gemstones: pearl, malachite, topaz, agate, calcite, aquamarine
Living Creatures: salmon, hare, seal, seagull, duck, whale, otter, beaver
Time of Day: 8:30 AM – 9:30 AM
Time of Year: October 16th – November 7th, April 29th – May 14th
Moon Phase: waxing
Astrology: Moon, Taurus, Aquarius, Mercury
Tarot: Moon, Star, Temperance
Sacred Objects: cup, cauldron, scrying bowl with water
Nine Worlds: Svartálfar
Zone: Material Earth Space
Magical Beings: water nymphs, merpeople, nixies, water elves
Hávamál's Rune Poem (Ljóðatal): 159
Magical and Meditative Practices: working with dreams and visions, developing and trusting in one's intuition., increasing psychic powers, calming anger, loosening tension, magnetizing situations, helping with sleep, seeing through deceptions and illusions, sexual magic, tapping into higher insights, strengthening aura, initiation into higher life, enlightenment of the ego, gaining higher understandings, aligning with the Wyrd, lunar mysteries, water magic and healing, trusting self, letting go of unhealthy behaviors, connecting with intuition

Rune Yoga: reflecting on all the streams of your life and seeing what it has manifested (adjust if needed), purification, emotional healing and growth, seeing and experiencing life through different perspectives, connecting with water, divination, defining and refining perspectives and beliefs, honing imagination, dream work, seeking visions

Associations: lake, water journey, emotions, feelings, self-discovery, desires, unconscious drives, compulsions, inward journey, introspection, sub-consciousness, intuition, receptivity, flow, water, urges, past, memories, mother, security, creativity, fluidity, ebb and flow, cleansing, knowing, psychic powers, peace, blessings, healing, Seiðr, concentrated imagination, transmitting, transmuting, subtle influences, dreams, love, life, flexibility, sympathy, empathy, seas, moisten, wave mechanics, life force, growth, properties of water, nourishing, mead, milk, law, restoration, laughter, loftiness, lightness, insights, spring, learning, initiation, experiences, vitality, deeper unknown and mystical forces, source of life, abundance, renewal, magnetism, rebirth

Adverse Associations: war, cessation of law and order, succumb to temptations, denial, astral damage, nightmares, fear, bad habits, negative patterns, avoidance, withering, emotionally imbalanced, false intuition, weak imagination, caught in illusions/delusions, day-dreaming, depression, emotional turmoil

INGWAZ

Pronunciation: ing-waz
Sound: *ing (gardening)*
Meaning: Ing, sacred land
Number: 3:6/22
Poem:

Old English
> Ing was first seen among the East-Danes
> as he passed by and continued eastward;
> across the waves, his wagon followed,
> thus these warriors named the hero.

Ideograms: seed, sacred space
Visualization: sacred space on fertile land
Divinities: Yngvi-Freyr, Nerthus
Eddas, Sagas, and Stories: King Yngvi of Sweden
Freyr Kennings: slayer of Beli, giver of peace, Njörðr's son
Healing: genitals, fertility issues
Direction: east
Color: yellow,
Elements: earth, water
Plants: gentian, barley, heal-all
Tree: apple
Incense: fennel
Gemstones: amber, ivory, topaz, jasper, malachite
Living Creatures: honeybee, owl, boar
Time of Day: 9:30 AM – 10:30 AM
Time of Year: May 14th – June 14th
Moon Phases: new, dark moon
Astrology: Venus, Capricorn, Aquarius

Tarot: Judgment
Sacred Objects: wagon, ship, grain, treasures, Idunn's apples
Nine Worlds: Vanaheim
Magical Beings: light elves
Magical and Meditative Practices: seeking and experiencing inner harmony and peace, overcoming illusions, healing mental illness, problem solving, calming, centering, promoting fertility and receptivity, storing energy, storing and transforming energy, fertility
Rune Yoga: self-actualizing, unifying energies, seeking internal and external harmony
Associations: possession, fertility, pleasure, gratification, empowering, gestation, introspection, digging at the roots, bigger picture, wholeness, potency, strength, body awareness, transformation, creative power, completion, new beginning, peace, bounty, sensuality, DNA chain, germination, growth, parenthood, integration, unity, fortunate, expansion, wealth, intuitive energy, seed, harmony, share, wanting to be desired, resolution, release from tension, potential energy, internal growth, self-replenishing, spiritual path, creative spark, happiness, pleasure, fulfillment, fertilization, movement, action, realization, vulva, female sexuality
Adverse Associations: impotence, scattered movement, infertile, bad ground and environment, unhealthy, decay and rottenness, uncertainty, stress

DAGAZ

Pronunciation: dah-gaz
Sound: *d (day)*
Meaning: day
Number: 3:7/23
Poem:

Old English
    Day is god's messenger,
    a source of hope and happiness
    to the rich and poor;
    beloved by all and a benefit to all alike.

Ideograms: sideways hourglass, infinity symbol, solar shield glasses to watch eclipse
Visualization: daylight
Divinities: Baldr, Dag, Óðinn, Ostara, Heimdall, Syn, Loki, Surt
Eddas, Sagas, and Stories: Shinfaxi and Hrimfaxi, Baldr's death and return, Sigrdrífa Hailing of the Day
Healing: sight
Direction: east
Colors: white, light blue, blue
Elements: fire, air, light
Plants: marigold, cowslip, St. John's wort, clary sage
Trees: whitebeam, oak, spruce, willow
Incense: clary sage
Gemstones: diamond, fluorite
Living Creatures: wren, butterfly, rooster
Time of Day: dawn, noon, 10:30 AM – 11:30 AM
Time of Year: Spring, May 29th – June 14th

Moon Phase: 1st quarter
Astrology: Sun, North Node
Tarot: Temperance
Sacred Object: scepter
Magical Beings: light elves
Magical and Meditative Practices: clarity, enlightenment, inviting serenity and contentment, deep insights and realization, transcendence, invisibility, mystical inspiration, cultivation positive thinking, radiating charisma
Rune Yoga: seeking fulfillment, being fully present in the moment, taking advantage of all opportunities, seeking and embodying wisdom, transforming energies
Associations: warmth, light, day, blessings, enlightenment, insight, transition time, synthesis, transcendence, mystical unity, increase, growth, illumination, left/right brain, healing, focus, understanding, eternity symbol, moebius strip, cataclysmic change, nuclear fission, nuclear winter, catalyst, between worlds, invisibility, spiritual welfare, transformation into highest self, cosmic consciousness, shape-shifting, ego, strength, intuition, major shift, right timing, outcome assured, self-trust, seize the moment, period of achievement and prosperity, dispelled darkness, breakthrough, visible spectrum, polarity, awareness, hope, happiness, ideal, clarity, certainty, balance, accountability, being fully present and enjoying life
Adverse Associations: lack of vision, lethargy, blindness, hopelessness, in the dark, ignorance

OTHALA

Pronunciation: oh-tha-lah
Sound: *o (home)*
Meaning: inheritance, with emphasis on inherited land
Number: 3:8/24
Poem:

Old English
    An estate/inheritance is dear to all
    who justly enjoys the blessings of home
    and the continual prosperity that flows with it.

Ideogram: sacred land of Ingwaz with roots
Visualization: being together with family to celebrate and enjoy life and to honor ancestors
Divinities: Óðinn, Ostara, Hertha
Eddas, Sagas, and Stories: Hávamál 36, Flateyjarbók, King Hroft's inheritance (King Hrolf Kraki's Sage, 25)
Healing: chest, back, neck
Direction: north
Colors: goldish green, light violet, light blue, light greenish yellow, deep yellow
Element: earth
Plants: snowdrop, goldthread
Trees: oak, hawthorn
Incense: marjoram
Gemstone: petrified wood, ruby, topaz
Living Creatures: stork, fish, eagle
Time of Day: 11:30 AM – 12:30 PM
Time of Year: February 26th – March 20th, June 14th – June 29th
Moon Phase: full

Astrology: Saturn, Mars, Scorpio, Taurus, Moon, Mercury
Tarot: Emperor, Moon
Sacred Object: treasure, throne
Zone: Material Earth Space
Magical Beings: land wights, hobgoblins
Magical and Meditative Practices: inviting peace and prosperity, protecting land and home, setting energetic roots, grounding, honing talents and skills, winning, growing spiritual power, raising mental energy, building the strength of one's word until what you say becomes reality, seeing and understanding genetic inheritance
Rune Yoga: finding wholeness and completion, manifesting energies at will, building strong family, having something of value to pass along
Associations: retreat, inheritance, property, acquisition, benefits, separating paths, letting go of the old, genetic inheritance, centering, grounding, kin, heritage, fundamental values, home life, above, beyond, ancestral country, nature, being, treasure, bringing about increase, persistent effort, nobility, guide, skill, formations, group prosperity, productivity, interaction, legacies, reputation
Adverse Associations: misuse, misunderstood, sickness, impotence of speech, dangerous situation, disorder, totalitarianism, slavery, poverty, homelessness, separation, submission

BIBLIOGRAPHY

Andersson, Theodore. M. and Kari Ellen Gade. *Morkinskinna*. Cornell University Press, 2012. Print.

Aswynn, Freya. *Northern Mysteries & Magick: Runes & Feminine Powers*. Woodbury, MN: Llewellyn Publications, 2009. Print.

Atwater, P. M. H. *Goddess Runes: Instructions in Brief*. Charlottesville, VA: P.M.H. Atwater, 2003. Print.

Atwater, P.M.H. *The Magical Language of Runes*. Bear & Company, 1990. Print.

Auden, W.H. and Paul Taylor. *Norse Poems*. Athlone Press, 1981. Print.

Avery, Aelfric. *Armanen Runes and the Black Sun Vol. I, II, & III*. Woodharrow Gild Press, 2018. Print.

Blum, Ralph. *The Book of Runes: A Handbook for the Use of an Ancient Oracle*. New York, NY: St. Martin's, 2008. Print.

Brink, Stefan and Neil Price. *The Viking World*. Routledge, 2011. Print.

Byock, Jesse L. *The Prose Edda*. Penguin Classics, 2006. Print.

Byock, Jesse L. *The Saga of King Hrolf Kraki*. Penguin Clasics, 1999. Print.

Byock, Jesse L. *The Saga of the Volsungs*, Penguin Classics, 2000. Print.

Byock, Jesse L. *Viking Age Iceland*. Penguin Books, 2001. Print.

Chamberlain, Lisa. *Runes for Beginners*. Chamberlain Publications, 2018.

Corby, Dana. *The Witches' Runes*. Amazon, 2018. Print.

Christiansen, Eric. *The Norsemen in the Viking Age*. Wiley Blackwell, 2001. Print.

Davidson, Hilda Ellis. *Gods and Myths of Northern Europe*. Penguin Books, 1965. Print.

Davidson, Hilda Ellis. *Myths and Symbols in Pagan Europe*. Syracuse University Press, 1989. Print.

Davidson, Hilda Ellis and Peter Fisher. *Saxo Grammaticus: The History of the Danes*. Boye6, 2008. Print.

Dee, Jonathan. *The Nordic Book of Runes*. Ryland Peters & Small Ltd., 2021. Print.

Denny, Michael William. *Rune Shamanism: The Forgotten Method of Galdor*. CreateSpace Independent Publishing, 2013. Print.

Eason, Cassandra. *The Little Bit of Runes*. Sterling Ethos, 2018. Print.

Elliot, Ralph. *Runes: An Introduction*. Manchester University Press, 1989. Print.

Faulkes, Anthony and George Johnson. *Three Icelandic Outlaw Sagas*. Orion Publishing Group, 2001. Print.

Flowers, Stephen E. *Runes and Magic: Magical Formulaic Elements in the Older Runic Tradition*. Smithville, TX: Runa-Raven, 2010. Print.

Foster, Justin. *Huld Manuscript*. Academia.edu, 2015. Print.

Foster, Justin. "Icelandic Magic Symbols (galdrastafir) and Spell Books (galdrabækur)". Academia.edu, 2015. Print.

Fries, Jan. *Helrunar: A Manual of Rune Magick*. Oxford: Mandrake, 1997. Print.

Frisvold, Nicholaj. *Trollrún: A Discourse on Trolldom and Runes in the Northern* Tradition. Hadean Press Limited, 2021. Print.

Gerrard, Katie. *Odin's Gateways*. Avalonia, 2011. Print.

Gitlin-Emmer, Susan. *Lady of the Northern Light: A Feminist Guide to the Runes*. Freedom, CA: Crossing, 1993. Print.

Grimnisson, Ruarik. *Rune Rede: Wisdom and Magick for the Life Journey*. Chieveley: Capall Bann, 2001. Print.

Harrell, Kelley. *Runic Book of Days*. Destiny Books, 2018. Print.

Helsdottir, Vervain. *Modern Rune*.: Rockridge Press, 2020. Print.

Herne, Wyldwood. *Anglo Saxon Rune Lore: A Brief Guide to the Anglo Saxon Runes*. Lulu, 2015. Print.

Hollander, Lee M. *Heimskringla*. University of Texas Press, 1964. Print.

Hollander, Lee M. *The Poetic Edda*. University of Texas Press, 1962. Print.

Howard, Michael. *The Magic of the Runes*. Rider, 1980. Print.

Howard, Michael. *The Wisdom of the Runes*. London: Rider, 1985. Print.

Hlynsson, Gunnar. *Norse Magic & Runes*. Amazon, 2021. Print.

Ingsson, Frodi. *Rune Yoga: Staða and Galdr*. Frodi Ingssson's Publishing, 2021. Print.

Kaldera, Raven. *The Pathwalker's Guide to the Nine Worlds*. Lulu, 2010. Print.

Karlsson, Thomas. *Nightside of the Runes: Uthark, Adulruna, and the Gothic Cabbala*. Inner Traditions, 2019. Print.

Kellogg, Robert, et al. *The Sagas of the Icelanders*. Penguin Classics, 2001. Print.

Kelly, Michael. *Aegishjalmur: The Book of Dragon Runes*. CreateSpace Independent Publishing, 2011. Print.

Kincaid, Ingrid. *Lost Teachings of the Runes*. Weiser Books, 2019. Print.

Kincaid, Ingrid and Lara Vesta. *The Runes Revealed: An (Un) Familiar Journey*. Ingrid Kincaid, 2020. Print.

King, Bernard. *Way of the Runes*. London: Thorsons, 2002. Print.

Knight, Sirona. *The Little Giant Encyclopedia of Runes*. Sterling Publishing, 2000. Print.

Krasskova, Galina. *Living Runes*. Weiser Books, 2019. Print.

Krasskove, Galina & Raven Kaldera. *Neolithic Shamanism*. Destiny Books, 2012. Print.

Krasskove, Galina & Raven Kaldera. *Northern Tradition for the Solitary Practitioner*. New Page Books, 2008. Print.

Krasskova, Galina. *Runes: Theory & Practice*. Franklin Lakes, NJ: New Page, 2010. Print.

Kummer, Siegfried Adolf. *Rune=magic*. Austin, TX: Runa-Raven, 1993. Print.

Kunz, Keneva. *The Vinland Sagas*. Penguin Classics, 2008. Print.

List, Guido, and Stephen E. Flowers. *The Secret of the Runes*. Rochester, VT: Destiny, 1988. Print.

Looijenga, Tineke. *Text & Contexts of the Oldest Runic Inscriptions*. Brill Academic Publication, 2003. Print.

MacLeod, Mindy and Bernard Mees. *Runic Amulets and Magic Objects*. Boydell Press, 2006. Print.

Mantius, Harold. *The Metaphysics of the Runes*. Amazon, 2018. Print.

Marby, Friendrich Bernhard. *Marby Runen-Bucherei*. Destiny, 1988. Print.

McCoy, Daniel. *The Viking Spirit*. CreateSpace, 2016. Print.

Meadows, Kenneth. *Rune Power: Make Sense of Your Life through the Wisdom of the Runes*. London: Rider, 2001. Print.

Morris, Simon. *The Runes of Evolution*. Templeton Press, 2015. Print.

Morris, William John Coles, et al. *Bandamanna Saga*. CreateSpace, 2012. Print.

Mountfort, Paul Rhys. *Nordic runes: understanding, casting, and interpreting the ancient Viking oracle*. Rochester, VT: Destiny , 2003. Print.

Museum of Icelandic Sorcery. *Rún: Magic Grimoire*. Strandaldur, 2014. Print.

Museum of Icelandic Sorcery. *Sorcerer's Screed*. Strandaldur, 2015. Print.

Olsen, Kaedrich. *Runes for Transformation: Using Ancient Symbols to Change Your Life*. San Francisco: Weiser, 2008. Print.

Osborn, Marijane, and Stella Longland. *Rune Games*. London: Routledge & K. Paul, 1982. Print.

Page, Raymond Ian. *Runes*. Los Angeles: U California, 1988. Print.

Page, Raymond Ian. *Runes and Runic Inscriptions*. The Boydell Press, 1998. Print.

Pálsson, Hermann and Paul Edwards. *Eyrbyggja Saga*. Penguin Classics, 1989. Print.

Palsson, Hermann and Paul Geoffrey Edwards. *Vikings in Russia*. Edinburgh University Press, 1989. Print.

Paxson, Diana L. *Taking Up The Runes: A Complete Guide To Using Runes In Spells, Rituals, Divination, And Magic*. Newburyport: Red Wheel Weiser, 2005. Print.

Pennick, Nigel. *Secret Lore Runes and other Ancient Alphabets*. Longon: Rider, 1991. Print.

Pennick, Nigel. *The Complete Illustrated Guide to Runes*. Greenwich Editions: London, 2003. Print.

Peschel, Lisa. *A Practical Guide to the Runes: Their Uses in Divination and Magick*. St. Paul, MN: Llewellyn Publications, 1999. Print.

Plowright, Sweyn. *The Rune Primer: A Down-to-earth Guide to the Runes*. United States: Lulu, 2006. Print.

Pollington, Stephen. *Rudiments of Runelore*. Norfolk: Anglo-Saxon, 1995. Print.

Price, Neil. *The Viking Way*. Oxbow Books, 2013. Print.

Rafnsson, Magnús. *Tvær Galdraskræður*. Srandagaldur, 2008. Print.

Rance, Suzanne. *The English Runes: Secrets of Magic, Spells and Divation*. Print.

RavenWolf, Silver, and Nigel Jackson. *Rune Mysteries: Companion to the Witches Runes*. St. Paul, MN: Llewellyn Publications, 2000. Print.

Simonds, Josh. *Beginner's Guide: Runes*. Rochridge Press, 2020. Print.

Short, William R. *Icelanders in the Viking Age*. McFarland & Company, 2010. Print.

Skjalden. "Nordic Culture." Nordic Culture, 25 May 2021, https://skjalden.com/.

Smith, Christopher. *Icelandic Magic. Aims, Tools, and Techniques*. Avalonia, 2016. Print.

Spiesberger, Karl. *Runenmagie*. Berlin: Schikowski, 1955. Print.

Spiesberger, Karl. Runenpraxis Der Eingeweihten *Runenexerzitien*. Richard Schikowski, 1982. Print.

Steffen, Kevin. *Runic States: The Shamanic Perception of Quantum Realities*. Eschaton. Print.

Storms, Godfrid. *Anglo-Saon Magic*. Springer, 1948. Print.

Thorsson, Edred. *Black Runa*. Asatrue Fok Assembly, 1995. Print.

Thorsson, Edred. *Blue Runa*. Asatrue Fok Assembly, 2011. Print.

Thorsson, *Edred. Futhark: A Handbook of Rune Magic*. Wellingborough: Aquarian, 1985. Print.

Thorsson, Edred. *Green Runa*. Asatrue Fok Assembly, 1996. Print.

Thorsson, Edred. *Icelandic Magic*. Inner Traditions, 2016. Print.

Thorsson, Edred. *Nine Doors Of Midgard: A Curriculum Of Rune-Work*. S.L.: Rune-Gild, 2016. Print.

Thorsson, Edred. *Rune Might: Secret Practices of the German Rune Magicians.* St. Paul, MN: Llewellyn Publications, 1994. Print.

Thorsson, Edred. *Runecaster's Handbook: The Well of Wyrd.* York Beach, Me. ;: Samuel Weiser, 1999. Print.

Thorsson, Edred. *Runelore: The Magic, History and Hidden Codes of the Runes.* San Francisco, CA: Weiser, 2012. Print.

Thorsson, Edred. *Rune-Song Book.* Asatru Fok Assembly, 2011. Print.

Thorsson, Edred. *The Galdrabook.* Runa-Raven, 2005. Print.

Tolkien, Christopher. *The Saga of King Heidrek the Wise.* Nelson's Icelandic Texts, 1960. Print.

Tyriel. *The Book of Rune Secrets.* James Stratton-Crawley, 2011. Print.

Tyson, Donald. *Rune Magic.* St. Paul, MN: Llewellyn Publications, 1999. Print.

Vesta, Lara Veleda. *Wild Soul Runes: Reawakening the Ancestral Feminine.* Weiser Books, 2021. Print.

Visconti, Sofia. *Runes: A Guide to the Magic Meanings.* Amazon, 2019. Print.

Waggoner, Ben. *A Pocket Guide to the Runes.* The Troth, 2019. Print.

Waggoner, Ben. *Norse Magical and Herbal Healing.* The Troth, 2011. Print.

Welz, Karl Hans. Basic Rune Course. www.magitech.com/runes.

Welz, Karl Hans. Basic Rune Course. www.magitech.com/runes.

Weor, Samael Aun. *The Gnostic Magic of the Runes: Gnosis, the Aeneid, and the Liberation of the Consciousness.* Brooklyn, NY: Glorian, 2008. Print.

Whitewolf, Isma. *The Runes of the Cosmic Goddess Course.* Amazon Digital Services LLC, 2013. Kindle.

Winroth, Anders. *The Age of the Vikings.* Princeton University Press, 2016. Print.

Wisehart, Troy & Andrea Wisehart. *Rise: Runes and Ritual.* Amazon, 2019. Print.

Wills, Tarrin. "Skaldic Project - Cross-Platform Interface." Skaldic Poetry of the Scandinavian Middle Ages, 27 July 2017, https://skaldic.org/.

Willis, Tony. *The Rune User's Handbook.* Wellingborough, Northamptonshire: Aquarian, 1987. Print.

Primary Internet Sources

www.runesecrets.net
www.runemaker.com
www.tirage-rune-magie.net
www.maginrose.com
www.soulintentarts.com/weekly-rune-gebo
www.germanenherz.blogspot.com
www.witchcircle-dtd.de
www.forstner-billau.at/Runen
www.elderfutharkrunes.blogspot.com
www.maginrose.com
www.kartarkasvatava-cz
www-witchcircle--dtd-de
www.hexerey-com
www.schamane--des--windes-com
www-wirkendekraft-at
www-felag--asatru-org
www.lokis-mythologie.de

GLOSSARY

Ægishjálmr The Helm of Awe was first mentioned in the Eddic poem Fáfnismál. The story of the Helm is expounded on in chapter 20 of the Volsung Saga. It gives the keeper victory over others. One spell collected from Jón Árnason instructs the user to carve the symbol on lead and press it onto their forehead while saying a specific formula.

Æsir tribe of Norse gods who formed Miðgarðr with Ymir's body and who often fight against the giants and their chaotic ways. Some of the major gods and goddess are Óðinn, Thor, Frigga, Baldur, Heimdall, Iðunn, Tyr, and Sif.

Ætt (plural aettir) family or group. In the Runic system there are three families of 8 Runes.

Alerunes carved Runes usually for protection and healing.

Álfheim home world of the elves.

Armanen Runes 18 Runes Guido von List ascribed to Óðinn's 18 Rune spells in the Hávamál 147-165.

Ásgarðr home world of the Æsir.

Althing general assembly where disputes and laws were settled

Ask first man as an ash tree is given breath, intelligence, warmth, motion, and soul by Óðinn and his brothers (Gylfaginning, 9).

Asyniur collective term for Norse goddesses

Auðumbla primordial cow that fed Ymir and who licked Búri (grandfather of the Æsir) out from the salty rime.

Berserkr warrior who channels, embodies, and energetically transforms into powerful animals during battle, most often bears.

Bifröst Rainbow Bridge connecting Miðgarðr to Ásgarðr.

Bindrune two or more Runes combined for magical, meditative, or secretive purposes.

Blót sacred gathering to honor and give offerings to god(s), goddess(s), ancestor(s), or wight(s). Traditionally the blood of the sacrificed animal was sprayed on statues, walls, participants, and the land.

Bracteate thin piece of engraved gold, sometimes with a loop to be worn on a necklace.

Brísingamen Freya's magical necklace.

Dísir guardian female spirit.

Embla first woman as an elm tree is given breath, intelligence, warmth, motion, and soul by Óðinn and his brothers (Gylfaginning, 9).

Fetch/Fylgja a part of the soul that is often projected as an animal.

Galdr Runic intonations used in spells and incantations through the process of working with vibrational energy.

Ginnungagap primal void.

Goði leader with political and religious roles in the community.

Hallow to consecrate and make sacred through ritual purification.

Hamingja a part of the soul connected with luck, often thought of as a personal entity that can be moved by will.

Hamr a part of the soul that gives shape/form to the body, but more mutable than the fixed appearance of the physical body (Lyke). Essential towards shapeshifting.

Hel a region in the world Niflheimr where many go after death.

Hugr the part of the soul dealing with the mind.

Jötunheimr home world of the giants.

Kenning poetic expression or phrase that generally alludes to some noun. Example: sea-steed for ship.

Lyke physical body.

Magic: using energy to bring about a chosen outcome.

Miðgarðr Middle Earth where humans live.

Mjölnir Thor's hammer.

Minni connected with memory.

Muspelheim world of the fire giants and Surtr.

Níðhöggr dragon gnawing at Yggdrasil's roots.

Níðstang a nithing pole made from a wooden staff with a horse's head placed on top and its skin laid over the pole to curse someone (Egil's Saga, 20).

Niflheimr dark, misty world where Hel resides.

Norns deities known to shape human fate.

Od life-force energy surrounding and within all things.

Ond life breath.

Ørlög "primal layers" that shape and defines our lives. Some of these layers are those things passed down to us such as genetics and luck, our past actions in this and previous lives, circumstances of life, actions dealt out to us by others, and larger and more powerful forces such as nature.

Ragnarök final battle of the gods with the chaotic forces.

Rune Yoga system of working with the body's energies towards self-cultivation and actualization.

Seiðr type of magic introduced to the Æsir by Freya.

Sigrún "victory rune."

Svefnþorn "sleep thorn" is used to put and keep someone asleep until the spell is broken or runs its course. .

Stave magical symbols similar to sigils.

Sumbel ritualized toast during feasts and sacred gatherings.

Svartálfaheimr home of the dark elves "dwarves' world.

Útiseta "sitting out" under a cloak as a ritualized meditation.

Vættir/Wight magical beings such as nature, house, and barrows spirits.

Valhalla "Hall of the Dead," where Óðinn's chosen reside until Ragnarök.

Valkyries "Choosers of the Fallen" are beings who influence battles and take great warriors slain in battle to abide and train in Valhalla until Ragnarök.

Vanaheimr world of the Vanir.

Vanir tribe of gods associated with fertility, magic, wisdom, and nature. Some of the major gods and goddesses are Njörðr, Freya, Freyr, and Nerthus.

Völva Norse practitioner of seiðr.

Wyrd that aspect of fate/destiny that is somewhat in our control, in that we weave our personal Wyrd through our words and deeds. The fact that past words and deeds are already woven means we have to deal with the consequences, and those consequences are not often in our control. Weaving our Wyrd does not happen with the snap of the fingers. We are already moving in a specific direction due to Ørlög and our past choices, like a massive ship in a channel, it isn't easy turning things around.

Yggdrasil the great cosmic tree connecting the Nine Worlds and all of life together.

Ymir came into being when the fires of Muspelheim and the icy world of Niflheimr neared each other in the great void of Ginnungagap. This unconscious hermaphroditic being's offspring were giants and dwarves. Ymir's body became the material that formed Miðgarðr.

INDEX

Associations

abilities, 16, 28, 65, 72

abundance, 15, 16, 36, 49, 75

achievement, 19, 49, 59, 79

actualizing, 77

archetypes, 19

assimilating, 22

astral, 10, 27, 51, 62, 68, 75

attractiveness, 62

authority, 31, 63

aware, 16, 31, 45, 46

awareness, 12, 16, 25, 36, 39, 45, 46, 48, 71, 72, 77, 79

balance, 27, 28, 33, 43, 46, 49, 57, 62, 63, 72, 79

balancing, 33, 39, 71

banishing, 30, 42, 48, 51, 52, 71

beginnings, 16, 65

beliefs, 43, 75

bindrune, 7, 8

birth, 53, 54, 55, 64, 65

bliss, 36

boundaries, 21, 28, 33, 39, 43, 46, 68

Astrology

Deities, Ancestors, & Magic Beings

Stones and Metals

ABOUT THE AUTHOR

Frodi lives in the Evergreen State with his wife and two youngest. He spends his free time homeschooling, playing in the garden, dancing with his love, hanging with friends, learning new skills, writing, and giving thanks for all the blessings in life. To learn more about the author and his path check out his book, *Rune Yoga: Staða and Galdr*.